ROUTLEDGE LIBRARY EDITIONS:
THE ECONOMICS AND POLITICS OF OIL
AND GAS

Volume 10

PROSPECTS FOR THE
WORLD OIL INDUSTRY

PROSPECTS FOR THE WORLD OIL INDUSTRY

Edited by
TIM NIBLOCK AND RICHARD LAWLESS

Routledge
Taylor & Francis Group

LONDON AND NEW YORK

First published in 1985 by Croom Helm Ltd

This edition first published in 2016
by Routledge
2 Park Square, Milton Park, Abingdon, Oxon OX14 4RN

and by Routledge
711 Third Avenue, New York, NY 10017

Routledge is an imprint of the Taylor & Francis Group, an informa business

British Library Cataloguing in Publication Data
A catalogue record for this book is available from the British Library

ISBN: 978-1-138-64127-3 (Set)
ISBN: 978-1-315-62232-3 (Set) (ebk)
ISBN: 978-1-138-64803-6 (Volume 10) (hbk)
ISBN: 978-1-315-62667-3 (Volume 10) (ebk)

Publisher's Note
The publisher has gone to great lengths to ensure the quality of this reprint but points out that some imperfections in the original copies may be apparent.

Disclaimer
The publisher has made every effort to trace copyright holders and would welcome correspondence from those they have been unable to trace.

Prospects for the World Oil Industry

Edited by TIM NIBLOCK and RICHARD LAWLESS

(Proceedings of a Symposium on the Energy Economy co-sponsored by the Petroleum Information Committee of the Arab Gulf States and the University of Durham, England, and held in Durham, 9-10 May 1984.)

CROOM HELM
London • Sydney • Dover, New Hampshire

© 1985 Tim Niblock and Richard Lawless
Croom Helm Ltd, Provident House, Burrell Row,
Beckenham, Kent BR3 1AT
Croom Helm Australia Pty Ltd, First Floor, 139 King Street,
Sydney, NSW 2001, Australia

British Library Cataloguing in Publication Data

Prospects for the world oil industry: (proceedings of a symposium on the energy
    economy co-sponsored by the Petroleum Information Committee of the Arab
    Gulf States and the University of Durham, England, and held in Durham,
    9-10 May 1984)
    1. Petroleum industry and trade
    I. Niblock, Timothy   II. Lawless, Richard I.
    III. Petroleum Information Committee of the Arab Gulf States
    IV. University of Durham
    338.2'7282   HD9560.5

ISBN 0-7099-4104-8

Croom Helm, 51 Washington Street,
Dover, New Hampshire 03820, USA

Library of Congress Cataloging in Publication Data

Symposium on the energy economy (1984: Durham, Durham)
    Prospects for the world oil industry

    1. Petroleum industry and trade—congresses.
    2. Gas industry—congresses.
    I. Niblock, Timothy   II. Lawless, Richard I.
    III. Petroleum Information Committee of the Arab Gulf States
    IV. University of Durham   V. Title
    HD9560.5.S96   1984   338.2'7282   85-4186

    ISBN 0-7099-4104-8

Phototypeset by Words and Pictures Limited, London SE19
Printed and bound in Great Britain by
Biddles Ltd, Guildford and King's Lynn

CONTENTS

Opinions published in this volume are those of the contributors and should not be construed as necessarily reflecting those views held by the Petroleum Information Committee of the Arab Gulf States or the University of Durham, England.

INTRODUCTION

by Professor F.G.T. Holliday (Chairman)
Vice-Chancellor and Warden, University of Durham, Durham, England

The Great Castle is the oldest part of the University of Durham and for about 900 years has been the gathering place for many distinguished visitors. For the last 150 years or so most visitors to this Castle have come with but one purpose in mind — to advance learning and understanding and that indeed is the purpose of our meeting here in Durham.

The Petroleum Information Committee of the Arab Gulf States is the primary sponsor of our gathering and it has been a great privilege for the University's Centre for Middle Eastern and Islamic Studies to have co-operated with the Committee in the organisation of this Symposium.

Last month the Chancellor of the Exchequer of the British Government asked 'What are we going to do when the oil runs out?' Personally, I think there is a more important topic to discuss — 'What are we going to do with the large amounts of oil and gas that are available to us?' The reserves of the Arab Gulf region are vast and even our own relatively modest supplies in the North Sea and associated basins will continue to come into the refineries and pipelines of the world well into the next century.

The pressing problems are not so much those of supply, as those of utilisation; utilisation not only of the oil and gas but also utilisation of the cash flows that they generate and utilisation of the skills that the industry has fostered in engineers and scientists.

There are dangers too. Perhaps the greatest danger is that this great industry which is trading in the very substance of our countries will, through lack of proper planning, or the misreading of the markets, or through ill-conceived national protectionism, bring itself into a state of instability and waste of opportunities. If the oil and gas industry falters the whole world falters with it. There seems to me to be no need for such an outcome. The world is a big market place and many countries have desperate needs for petrochemicals and their products.

2   *Introduction*

This Symposium, by discussing these important matters in the very peaceful city of Durham, can help both suppliers and consumers make best use of one of the world's greatest assets.

OPENING ADDRESS

His Excellency Sheikh Nasser Mohammed Al-Ahmed Al-Jaber Al-Sabah
Under Secretary—Chairman of Petroleum Information Committee, Ministry of Information, Kuwait

It is a pleasure to speak to you again on the opening of this Symposium on behalf of my colleagues who honour me to take this stand today.

I should like, first of all, to express my deep gratitude to the University of Durham for its kind invitation to co-sponsor this Symposium on Arabian Gulf/European Interactions. Many thanks also to the Organising Committee of this Symposium on both sides.

I cordially welcome all participants. Your presence here and quality show how important it is to meet together today to explore new opportunities for co-operation.

Our Symposium today is the fourth in a series of similar Euro-Arab Symposia which our Petroleum Information Committee for the Arab Gulf States (PIC) began in 1981. As you know, the Arab Gulf States in historical terms must rate as one of the newest energy producing areas in the world. The petroleum industry throughout the Arab Gulf States is of comparatively recent origin, to be seen in terms of a few decades.

Arriving in Durham, we come to one of the oldest energy areas in the world. This thought prompts me to reflect on how interlinked our interests are today, and indeed how interlinked we shall continue to be for foreseeable decades.

In the Gulf we have heard of your famous Durham Miners' Gala Day, held once a year, when traditionally the leaders of the great British trade union movement gather here to celebrate this historic occasion. Everyone has heard of the Durham miner. And now, in the past few years we have been hearing still more regarding a new development, not many miles off the shores of Durham, which has added so greatly to Britain's energy resources. I speak, of course, of North Sea oil.

If I may, I will therefore dwell briefly on the important interrelationships between the separate energy resources of the Gulf region (oil and gas) and the energy resources of the United Kingdom (oil, gas, coal and indeed nuclear energy). First, let us make a comparison between your own ancient coal industry, typified by the activity in this industrial County of Durham, and the oil industry of our Arab Gulf States of Kuwait, Saudi Arabia, Bahrain, Qatar, the United Arab Emirates and Oman — now known as the Gulf Co-operation Council (GCC) — and Iraq. I propose to show how the oil industry of the Gulf has in fact also benefited the entire energy industry of Durham and the United Kingdom.

During the early 1970s when the price of oil was increased to bring it in line with market forces and other industrial commodities, it was often said in the Western media that the producing countries were attempting to put pressure on the consumers. Now, this was not the case. There is another way of looking at this issue; for example, take your own dynamic North Sea oil industry. This is another energy industry which has benefited the entire British nation. It largely solves the nation's balance of payments problems. It cushions the effects of world recession. It has become, from a governmental point of view, a beneficial tax payer of tremendous importance in maintaining your high standards of national life — from social service to defence. Yet it is very often forgotten that drilling would never have begun in the North Sea had the era of cheap oil been prolonged. In short, the oil price increase gave to you, our British friends, the opportunity to develop unused and previously unexplored energy resources.

Therefore, our view in the Arab Gulf and among the members of the Petroleum Information Committee is that we welcome other energy resources being developed be they oil, gas, nuclear or coal. For our oil is an expendable and depletable resource and we do not want to waste it. We are advocates of energy conservation — a factor often forgotten by those media and political critics who attempt to describe us as some form of 'exploiters' — a definition as distasteful to us as it would be to you if we were to describe any of your own energy resources — oil, coal or whatever — as exclusively exploitable.

Our message is co-operation. We seek more co-operation, not less, between the Arab Gulf States and your country, for example, your own North Sea oil industry. We see a comfortable world demand for OPEC oil especially from our region in the years ahead. You are in Britain, I note, currently producing around 2.5 million barrels per day. With these facts in mind, we want like you, to see a stable world energy industry, without disruptive price shocks. We want more co-operation, not less. Our friends in Mexico, for example, have recently been co-operating with our countries and we would, on the same terms, welcome great United Kingdom co-operation.

Co-operation means just what it says, and I refer to all fields in the Arab Gulf States. For example, we are entering the petrochemical market with high hopes and as a senior energy executive said recently (Ludovick von Wachen, Managing Director of Royal Dutch Shell group speaking at Cambridge International Energy Conference, 8 April 1984), 'Britain and Europe should be very cautious about restricting trade by erecting any barriers'. We need to co-operate in this as in other matters.

To sum up we want to achieve a prosperous future for our own people. And we want to achieve this continuously and steadily in friendly partnership with Europe and in particular with the United Kingdom and your own energy resources — oil, coal or nuclear energy. Co-operation is the very essence of the Arab language. We want to co-operate not confront. We need your technical skills, training programmes in oil and gas production, downstream operations, petrochemical technology and industry, research and development and so forth. We want to see a mutuality of interest in the vast market we continue to offer for your manufactured products and services. We want you to recognise the mutuality of interest we have, and the shared benefits we shall enjoy, in the development of our energy industries.

For true co-operation to take place, our international relationships have to be conducted in an atmosphere of stability and peace. Europe has developed and has achieved prosperity mainly because of an era of peace following the Second World War. Yet our Arab region has hardly seen any real peace. Part of our Arab population, namely the Palestinian people, are uprooted from their homeland, others are occupied by the Israeli forces, supplied and supported by the West. And in our own specific region a war has continued to rage for the last four years, in spite of all peace initiatives undertaken either from our side or by true friends. This war is serving no one's interests except the war beneficiaries.

Our brothers in Iraq have stated time and time again that their option is for peace but the other side is refusing to come to a sensible and just solution which the region and the world need.

We firmly believe that a real appraisal of the situation in the Middle East must be undertaken by the EEC countries collectively and in the light of the principles of law and justice, regardless of any new conditions created by armed forces belonging to either side of the conflicting parties. This will, no doubt, enhance the chances to secure peace for all in our region. The atmosphere of war and tension that has now prevailed for a long time in the Middle East is hardly conducive to the kind of collaboration which we are trying to promote. Those who think that oil, economics and trade can be separated from the realities of these conditions are wrong and have already been proven wrong if history is read carefully. Today, many of us in the Arab Gulf who have not given up hope for a peaceful solution to all these conflicts feel that Europe, and especially Britain, can play an important and effective role in achieving real peace for all in our region and the rest of the world.

We are trying to build modern states that need first and foremost the participation of the people in all aspects of life. So our urgent priority is to develop our human resources. We have, collectively, successfully achieved some of these aims especially in the fields of education, health and other social services but surely you realise that we have a long way to go and we need to mobilise all the resources at our disposal. Our traditions, culture and religion all motivate us to take extra care of human beings and we have our own successes and challenges. We would like you to understand that these challenges are great. But our Prophet told us that God will help those who endeavour to help others, and by others we mean the whole of mankind.

So let us co-operate and let this Durham Symposium at this historic University with its close links with the Middle East symbolise the spirit with which we can together iron out some or all of our problems.

Chairman

Thank you very much indeed, Your Excellency, for that truly magnificent opening address. If I may say so, it had all the marks of a speech of a statesman and it showed, I think you will all agree, a very deep insight into all of the many aspects of the energy economy. If I may say again, I valued particularly the way in which you drew the thread from the natural resource to the aspirations of people, to the need of the world for peace, and from there to the aspirations of people in terms of education and health.

Thank you again for a magnificent opening address.

Mr John Wiggins
Under Secretary and Head of Oil Division, Department of Energy,
London

Perhaps I might start by saying how much I endorse what Sheikh Nasser has said about the importance of building co-operation between us. This is something to which the British Government attaches the greatest importance. Perhaps I could spend five minutes or so making a few points which could serve as the background to our discussions today. Sheikh Nasser remarked that the Gulf oil industry was relatively new compared with the Durham coal mines and in a way I think one could also say that the UK oil industry was relatively new compared with what has been going on in the Gulf. The comparison is more or less exact: the Gulf is a thoroughly mature oil province just as Durham is a thoroughly mature coal field. In oil, Britain is still very much engaged in the business of exploration and development.

I think it behoves the British participants in this Symposium to bear in mind the enormous improvements in the Gulf oil industry. Production by the states which are members of the Gulf Co-operation Council is running at the moment at about 8½ to 9 million barrels per day, compared with UK production of 2½ million barrels per day. If you look at the figures of total world reserves of oil, and I suspect it is very difficult to get figures on which to base a comparison, about 50 per cent of all the discovered reserves lie in the Gulf area. United Kingdom reserves, even after the upgrading that we announced in the Brown Book published earlier this week, probably come to 15 to 20 billion barrels, whereas the Gulf States have proven reserves of 300 or 350 billion barrels. This is a factor of 20 times our reserves at least. The Gulf States could continue to produce at their present rate of production for most of the next century, I would suspect, whereas we in Britain will see our production beginning to decline by the end of this decade. Our endeavour will have to be to continue our exploration and development efforts so as to slow down that rate of decline. This is an experience which other major oil provinces like Canada, the United States and even the Soviet Union and Indonesia also face; in all those places the effort at the moment is to maintain production for as long as possible.

Sheikh Nasser has referred to the enormous impact which the oil industry has had on recent world economic history. It has brought about an enormous change — and I am not at all criticising this — in the world distribution of income, and it has forced the industrial countries to carry through enormous changes in their industrial structures, with which they are still having to come to terms. One has to admit that the changes, perhaps as in 1979/80, have had a big impact on the level of world economic activity ever since. In looking at all of these things we in Britain occupy a rather strange middle position between countries whose interests immediately and directly are very much concerned with the export of oil and those countries who only consume it and depend on it vitally for their industrial development. We in Britain for the time being are a small net exporter; this will obviously not continue for very many years. Unlike other oil exporters, we are also a mature industrial economy. Oil is a relatively small part of our gross domestic product — of the order of 5 per cent. Even of our tax revenues, the oil revenue, welcome though it is, only represents 8 or 9 per cent or something like that of government revenue. So we have to balance our interests as an oil producer with our interests as an oil consumer and as an integrated part of the Western industrial economy which the OECD organisation brings together. As Ministers in the British Government have repeatedly made clear over the last two or three years, we do very strongly favour the maintenance of as much stability as possible in the world oil market. I very much welcome what Sheikh Nasser said about avoiding further big price shocks; that is an objective which we very much share.

Perhaps I could also say one thing about the way in which we organise the oil industry. We, I think, maintain in this country the freest market in oil; unlike the United States, we maintain no restrictions over the export of oil. Although we produce substantially more than our own requirements, we do still continue to import a very substantial amount of oil from the Middle East and other parts of the world which happens to fit the configurations of our refineries. It makes good economic sense that we are able to export our light sweet crude oil and depend to a considerable degree still on heavier crudes, some of which are produced in the Gulf. This is an area in which the government has left the pattern of trading oil products to be entirely determined by the market. Similarly, in the exploration of our resources we do depend wholly on the very considerable group of private companies, both British and international, which have been responsible for the development of the resources of the North Sea. We do not have any sort of day-to-day or year-to-year control over the output they produce. Once the licensees have installed the facilities and provided they can satisfy us that they will be able to produce all the oil that is economically producible, we leave it to them to determine how much oil they are going to get out. We prevent them from flaring gas in a wasteful way and we prevent them from producing the oil so fast that they do reservoir damage, but we do not impose other controls.

Taking a parochial view of what we should be doing in the next few years, it is very clear that offshore exploration and development will continue at a very high level in the UK as it will in other parts of the North Sea and also I think in North America, China (now developing rapidly), West Africa and Indonesia. The challenge for us is to find the reserves in our own sector, to develop the technology which is needed to produce them economically and to produce in deeper water and smaller fields, and generally to cope with more difficult conditions and perhaps more difficult material. The development of oil and gas will remain an extremely important dynamic in British industrial activity in the foreseeable future — to the end of the century at the very least. There never was any prospect that oil production and the impact it has on the British economy would suddenly come to an end in 1990 as some commentators have started to think. Looking back on it, oil developed very suddenly as we found one or two very large fields that came on stream, but their production will tail off very gradually well into the next century. We are now doing our best to build up other production which will take the place of those fields as they come off plateau. The higher estimates of undiscovered reserves that we published this week obviously improve our confidence that we too will continue to be an active and successful oil province for some time to come. It is also very important to us that the technology which we have developed to cope with more difficult conditions than anywhere else in the world, to deal with the weather in the North Sea, should now be exported to other parts of the world where comparable conditions would be faced, say in maritime Canada. So we shall continue to have a vital interest in the success of the oil business, not only because of our own production but because of the impact which we hope our technology will be able to make on continuing activity world wide. I am very grateful for the opportunity to throw a few points into the discussion this morning.

Chairman

Thank you very much indeed for bringing the British oil and gas situation into the context of the larger reserves. I think it is important these days to keep in mind that even quite a small production, now in a sense acting on the margins, can tip the scales. I do not intend to say very much more but as the day goes on I would like us all to remember a story that appears in both the Koran and the Bible. It is a story of a dream — a dream of seven fatted cows and seven lean cows which devoured the fatted cows, and seven green ears of corn and seven others that were dry. It was the correct interpretation of that dream which saved a great civilisation and I think we ought to keep that in mind during the day.

DISCUSSION

Question

At present there appears to be a recovery of demand in the world oil market. In the first quarter of 1984, 36.4 billion barrels of oil were consumed in the OECD countries.

If we go back to January and February 1983 we see that the cut in prices which occurred then was based on the logic that demand had decreased. Britain at that time forced Nigeria to reduce the price of its light crudes by reducing the prices of its own North Sea crudes. So the whole structure of prices went down. Now that the situation has been reversed, it seems logical that the price should go up and there are already negotiations to bring this about. What, now, will be the position of Britain? Will it force Nigeria to keep its price at $US29 a barrel or will it allow the price to reflect increased demand?

Mr Wiggins asserts that the oil market is a free market, but 'free market' is a very strange term to use in this context. If Saudi Arabia allowed its production to go as high as it could, to ten million barrels per day, the pricing structure would collapse entirely — including the price for British crudes. The term 'free market' is not valid any more. There should be co-operation among all producers and this co-operation should take place right now so as to prevent prices from collapsing.

Chairman

I would first like Dr Al-Chalabi to respond to this.

Dr Al-Chalabi

I would like to take up just one point: that concerning the relevance of competitive market forces to OPEC's pricing policies. It is true that OPEC's $US5 reduction in its price last year stemmed from short-term pressures in the market following from the lowered pricing of North Sea and then Nigerian oil. The previous OPEC prices came under great pressure and finally OPEC just had to reduce its price. This, however, was not purely the result of market forces: OPEC could simply have decided to keep its price at $US34 by reducing production. In spite of Nigeria reducing its price, the other members of the organisation could, theoretically at least, have kept the price. I believe that in setting prices the oil producing countries and the oil industry generally should look not just at the short-term market forces, but also at the long-term effects of prices on the world supply/demand balance. The respective parts to be played by each one of the producing nations in the international oil trade also need to be considered. The simple increase of demand in the first quarter of 1984 does not by itself constitute a justification for raising the price. Pricing policy should serve long-term purposes; one of the longer-term objectives of pricing policy is to keep the market stable for as long as possible.

Mr Wiggins

I agree generally with what Dr Al-Chalabi has said. Sheikh Yamani made an extremely interesting speech in London in March 1982 when he said that the oil producers had allowed the oil price to go up too much in 1979/80. The responsibility for that price rise, however, did not rest entirely with the oil producers. It was also a question of foolishness on the part of the oil importers. In any case, the ultimate effect of that price rise was that the demand for oil went down and that in turn caused the fall in prices in 1983. There is in that respect, therefore, a free market which cannot be suppressed. If you are able to organise the producers, you may be able to control the price; but the volume of sales will then depend on what people are prepared to buy at that price. Decisions must be taken on that basis. I agree very much that the right thing to do in present circumstances is to hold the price steady while the world economy expands. This seems to me the best means of achieving a balanced economic development of both oil producers and oil consumers, and to represent the true path of co-operation.

Mr Barges H. Al-Barges
Chairman and Director General of Kuwait News Agency, Kuwait

In the name of Allah, the beneficent, the merciful.

In recent decades, the world has realised distinct progress in all walks of life. Although this achievement may pass into history as a source of pride for our generation, yet the lack of its generality is by all means a great mishap, for which we all have to share the blame.

The fact that this progress is not shared on a global level is in serious contravention to all noble ideals and human values. When such a success is not utilised in serving the cause of prosperity and the common good, that means a certain group of people has elected to exploit science and technology to serve their own ends without regard to others.

The people on this planet are in unanimous agreement that the era of colonisation is gone for ever and it is now time to live together in an atmosphere of fraternity, co-operation and friendship. There is general agreement, too, on a constant search to realise a decent living for everybody, everywhere. Otherwise the world will remain a jungle where the weak are victimised by the strong, the rich become richer and the poor are left poorer.

As a result of the historical and unprecedented progress in communications, the world became a small spot. This means that co-operation for creating a better world is no longer a difficult task. To realise such an objective, members of the international community should cease to be self-centred and to refrain from all acts of discrimination. All of us, each in his field, should exert every possible effort in formulating a new world where peace, security and prosperity shall prevail.

Such efforts should be made within the frameworks of the United Nations charter and other international conventions. We should ascertain that our agreements and pledges in that respect are implemented so that we will not continue to face turmoils, injustice and poverty.

May you permit me, in my capacity as Chairman of the Kuwait News Agency and President of the Federation of Arab News Agencies, to address this honourable gathering on the role that could be played by the information media.

In the world of today, the information system is enjoying new facilities which were made possible by the accurate, speedy and diversified means of communications. Despite all these advantages and the professional ethics set to govern media performance, the system has not, so far, succeeded in realising its anticipated objectives. This is perhaps due to its failure to overcome self-motivations. To play an honest role, the information media needs nothing more than strict observation of its own professional principles.

Taking the elements of reality and justice into consideration, we will begin to head towards realising all the noble human objectives. Media men should remain constantly committed to objectivity and honesty. They should concentrate on causes beneficial to all people and refrain from handling issues that may cause frictions within their ranks.

It is indeed regrettable that the Western information system has for some time failed to abide by the principles laid for the profession. On many occasions, that media extended blind support to Western interests. In so doing, it tended to trade in excitement and in diverting people, including Westerners themselves, away from their real interests.

The Western media, for example, concentrated on the Arab-Israeli wars and in coverage of the fighting without any explanations as to the cause of that conflict. It made no efforts to expose the expulsion of an entire Arab people from its own land and the implanting of a foreign entity deep into Arab soil without mention to the injustice done to Palestinian Arabs who were being murdered and dispersed.

The Western media continued to concentrate on differences between nations, and, except in rare cases, it paid no attention to the cause of development or the relentless efforts of people to catch up with civilisation and to realise progress.

Throughout the years when Arab oil was sold at very cheap prices, while oil majors continued to extract substantial profits from its exploration and marketing, and the similar tax gains realised by Western governments, the information media remained silent.

When oil exporters, and not the Arabs alone, increased prices, the Western media created a turmoil for Arab producers, completely ignoring the enormous gains of the oil majors and Western governments who continued to draw more profits after the price increase which was dictated by supply and demand.

The Western media seems to have taken it for granted that the formula of supply and demand may be applied in Western countries but not in other regions. On the other hand, that media completely ignored the sharp increase in the cost of numerous commodities imported by Arabs and non-Arabs from Western markets.

It is only fair that Western consumers should be informed or made aware that, so far, oil exporting countries receive only 45 per cent of what they are paying for oil. Those same consumers should be told that their own governments and the oil majors are making more profits in that respect than the owners of the oil.

Furthermore, the Western media is paying no attention to the considerable assistance provided by oil producers, mostly Arab producers, to the developing world and international organisations, an assistance that by far exceeds all the aid contributions made by the advanced industrialised West.

The information media, let me say in conclusion, has a vital role towards the international community and to fulfil this role we have made several contacts and held various meetings either at bilateral levels between the Kuwait News Agency and other agencies of the world or in a collective manner between the Federation of Arab News Agencies and its European, Asian, African and Latin American counterparts.

We also held numerous and successful dialogues with newspapers and other media organisations around the globe, as part of the continued effort to create a system of free, honest and balanced information. The Federation will follow up the issue on a world-wide scale. We know there is a long way to go but let us always remember that a journey of 1,000 miles begins with one step.

I am pleased to say that efforts exerted by the Federation of Arab News Agencies are receiving a positive response and, in co-operation with other information groups, we will continue to participate in bringing together the views of all peoples and assert our adherence to peace, security, justice and prosperity and condemnation of all forms of discrimination, oppression and exploitation.

Chairman

Thank you very much indeed. You indeed remind us that the peoples of the world rely on the news media to inform and to interpret events and that there are great responsibilities placed on the news media. In discussions of the relationships between oil producers and consumers the news media should, as you so rightly stress, pay attention to the interest of all sides. Thank you.

THE PREDICTION OF STRATEGIC RESERVES

by Dr A.J. Martin
General Manager (Exploration) BP Petroleum Development Ltd,
London

The prediction of oil and gas reserves and future resources is fundamental to many governments' economic planning and to oil companies' exploration and investment policies. In the following paper, firstly, a brief outline is given of those geological factors whose assessment is essential to the prediction of hydrocarbon potential and, secondly, comments are made on the distribution of present proven reserves and future discoveries.

In order to simplify matters, only conventional hydrocarbon resources are discussed, that is, crude oil and natural gas. Natural gas liquids are noted. For definitions of the terms as used in this chapter, see below.*

This paper does not deal with non-conventional hydrocarbon resources such as tar-sands and oil-shales although it is recognised that theoretically large resources of these types exist in some countries.

---

*

Petroleum – a naturally occurring mixture of predominantly hydrocarbons in the gaseous, liquid or solid state.

Crude oil – the portion of petroleum that exists in the liquid phase in natural underground reservoirs and remains liquid at atmospheric conditions of pressure and temperature.

Natural gas – the portion of petroleum that exists in the gaseous phase or in solution in crude oil in natural underground reservoirs, and which is gaseous at atmospheric conditions of pressure and temperature.

Natural gas liquids – those portions of natural gas which are recovered as liquids. NGLs include condensate and liquefied petroleum gases but exclude liquefied natural gas (LNG).

Reserves – comprise proven and probable amounts of hydrocarbons remaining in the ground which can be extracted using current technology at costs considered economic in today's terms. Reserves therefore *do not* include:
(a) that portion of the in-place hydrocarbons which is not recoverable;
(b) hydrocarbons which will require extensive enhanced recovery projects but whose economic recovery has not been firmly established;
(c) hydrocarbons which have not yet been discovered.

In order to make realistic predictions of reserves and future discoveries it is necessary as a first step to have a clear understanding of the geological factors controlling the distribution and occurrence of hydrocarbons in the area under review. There are some basic and fundamental geological conditions which have to be satisfied before an oil or gas field can come into existence. Their assessment and prediction is at the heart of all hydrocarbon exploration.

For an oil or gas field to exist it is necessary to have three rock types present, namely a source rock, a reservoir rock and a cap-rock.

The source rocks are those from which the hydrocarbons are derived. They usually consist of fine grained shales or limestones in which residual organic debris has been trapped whilst the sediment was deposited. This organic debris is collectively known as kerogen (Figure 1.1). Under the right conditions it will give rise to a variety of hydrocarbons, the composition of which, from any one source rock, will depend upon the original character of the kerogen. Thus some source rocks will be oil prone and others gas prone.

Figure 1.1: Organic Material and Kerogen within the Oil Maturity Window

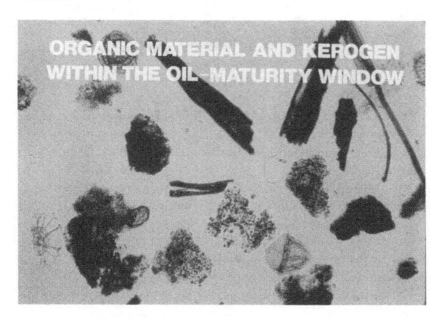

Reservoir rocks are those which contain the hydrocarbons and from which the oil and gas are produced. They usually consist of sandstones or limestones in which a significant pore-space exists

between the constituent grains of the rock in which the oil and gas is stored. The porosity of the rock determines the volume of liquid that can be held in the rock (Figures 1.2 and 1.3). There are no underground rivers or lakes of oil — it all lies within the pore-space of the reservoir rock.

Figure 1.2: Diagrammatic Section through a Sandstone Showing Liquids Held in the Inter-granular Pore Spaces

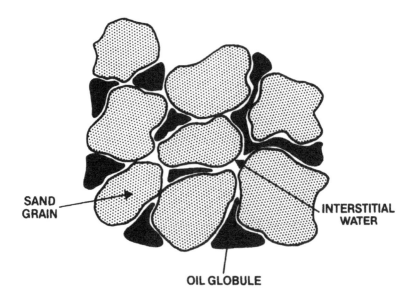

SAND GRAIN

INTERSTITIAL WATER

OIL GLOBULE

For a reservoir to be effective the pore spaces must be in communication with each other. This pore communication will determine the permeability and is essential to allow the fluids within the reservoir to move.

The cap-rock, in contrast to the reservoir rock, has to be composed of fine-grained material, often well compacted, with little or no porosity and permeability. This is the rock which retains the hydrocarbons within the reservoir and without which the oil and gas would escape to surface and be lost. Evaporites (gypsum and salt) or well indurated shales typify good cap-rocks.

The basic source, reservoir and cap-rock strata comprise part of the sedimentary rock suite. Such rocks were originally mostly sediments deposited in former seas, often as detritus derived from pre-existing land masses. Present day accumulations of sedimentary rocks, often as much as 10 km thick, are known as sedimentary basins and

Figure 1.3: Sandstone Reservoir in Thin-Section Showing Inter-granular Porosity

Figure 1.4: World Sedimentary Basins

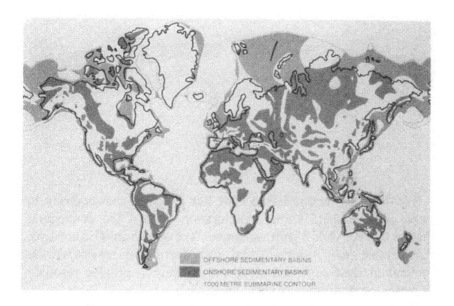

represent the sites of former seas. All known oil and gas deposits occur in such basins.

Thus the first step in the prediction of future hydrocarbon potential is to identify the sedimentary basins in which the requisite rock types noted above are known to occur. Since much of the sedimentary fill of these basins has been derived from the denudation of former continents the basins can be expected to form part of, or lie peripheral to, existing continents (Figure 1.4).

There is a fundamental difference between the geology of the continents and the deep oceans, elegantly expressed in recent years by the statement of the theory of Plate Tectonics (Figure 1.5). Consequently we look to the geology of the continents and their margins and not to the deep oceans for the identification of future hydrocarbon resources.

Figure 1.5: Generalised Section Across a Spreading Ocean Flanked by Continents

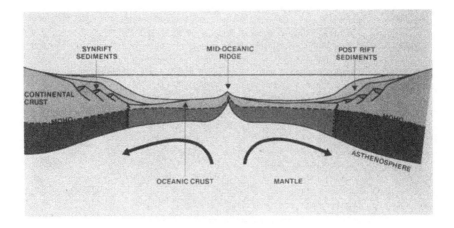

Exploration over the last decade has indicated that contrary to some opinions held earlier, exploration beyond the continental shelves will not yield significant amounts of oil and gas (Figure 1.6). Furthermore indications are that even deep-water regions on the continental shelf edge and slope are unlikely to provide resource increases proportionate to their area.

The presence of suitable basins and of the rocks mentioned above is in itself insufficient to give rise to oil or gas fields. There is a sequential

Figure 1.6: Sedimentary Sequences of a Continental Margin

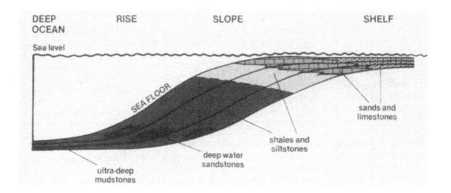

aspect to their occurrence that has to be satisfied in addition to that of simply being present. In other words the rocks must have been deposited in the correct order to be effective. Thus the source rock has to be in contact with the reservoir rock to allow the hydrocarbons, when expressed from the source rock, to have access to the reservoir. The cap-rock, if it is to retain the hydrocarbons, must have been deposited after the reservoir rock. Clearly an impermeable stratum underlying a reservoir will be useless as a cap-rock. Thus a reservoir rock has to be in place and sealed at the time of hydrocarbon generation and migration if the trapping system is to work.

The tectonic history, as well as the sedimentation history, of a sedimentary basin is a critical factor in the formation of oil fields. It is necessary for the strata to have been folded and/or faulted into configurations which form effective traps. Many variations of trap types occur. They often show a combination of structural, strati-graphic and sedimentological factors which all add to the problem of forecasting field presence and size (Figure 1.7).

A source rock is only effective if sustained tectonic subsidence ensures it has been buried to sufficient depth long enough for the hydrocarbons to have been formed by heat and to have been expressed by pressure from the rock. Conversely, if held at high temperatures for too long the source rock will be spent. With

Figure 1.7: Sketch Diagram of Hydrocarbon Trap Types

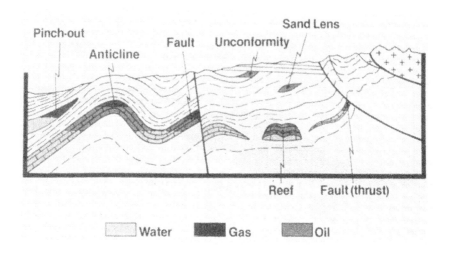

increasing burial and associated increasing temperatures the hydro-carbons generated will become increasingly gas prone (Figure 1.8). Thus there is a greater likelihood of finding gas in deep prospects. However each sedimentary basin has its own 'hydrocarbon floor', below which no hydrocarbons will occur as any that remain trapped at excessive depths will be destroyed. Most oil and gas occurs in rocks of Upper Mesozoic to Lower Tertiary age deposited some 210 to 25 million years ago. These rock sequences are now at their optimum development for hydrocarbon generation and entrapment. Those that are younger are generally immature and lack trap configuration. Pre-existing traps in older rocks tend to have been destroyed by erosion or secondary tectonic events, particularly faulting (Figure 1.9).

In short the geological conditions that need to be satisfied before prediction can begin are: (a) locate suitable sediment accumulations, (b) determine that rocks have been deposited in a correct sequence, (c) ascertain if the source rocks can have generated part or all of their hydrocarbon potential, (d) if oil and gas are available in the system determine that a migration path to the reservoir existed, and (e) at the time of migration the reservoir was in an effective trap configuration (Figure 1.10).

If these conditions are all satisfied then an oil or gas field may well exist. Identification of this sequence of rock types and geological

Figure 1.8: Generation of Hydrocarbons with Depth and Temperature

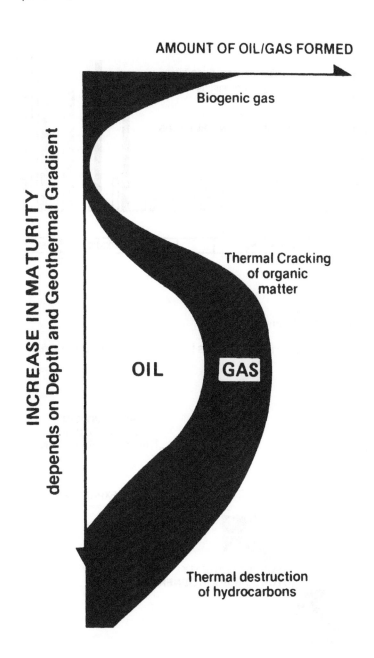

Figure 1.9: Giant Oil Fields — Geological Age of Reservoirs

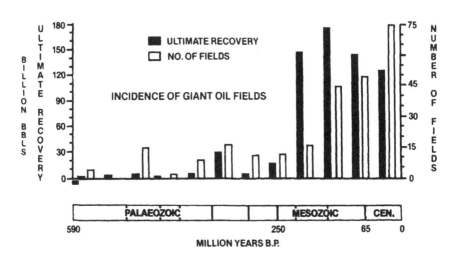

Source: From J.D. Moody.

Figure 1.10: Sequence of Events Leading to the Formation of an Oil or Gas Field

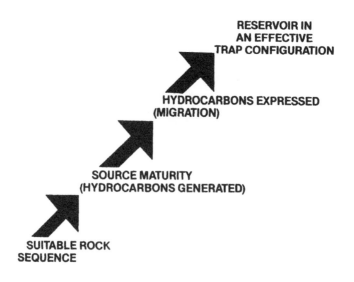

events, basin by basin, country by country, followed by the search for the actual fields, forms the basis of the whole of the oil and gas exploration business. The regional assessment of sedimentary basins by the oil industry has been intensive over the years. There are few basins that, either for logistical or for political reasons, have not been explored to some degree. The immensity of the data base which the industry can now use cannot be overemphasised. Hand in hand with this it must also be emphasised that as large as the data base is the final prediction and assessment of the presence and size of hydrocarbon accumulations is a subjective interpretation and judgement. In spite of the enormous geological effort made today the prediction of future discoveries contains many uncertainties which remain unresolved until wells are drilled. The world-wide exploration success ratio today is about 1:10, and even after discovery a field requires extensive appraisal drilling before its size can be truly assessed. Herein lies the exploration risk which is present in every exploration forecast.

The distribution of oil and gas around the world should now be considered. Fortunately naturally occurring hydrocarbons are not uncommon minerals and no doubt much greater quantities have been generated and lost by natural causes than have been trapped. The estimates for discovered hydrocarbons show a fair agreement among various authors and the main element of uncertainty is the recovery factor which has been used to arrive at the reserve figures quoted. Much greater variations exist between authors when dealing with future discoveries. Even in this field opinions are generally closer than they were a decade ago (Figure 1.11).

The figures which follow are essentially the British Petroleum Company's view of world hydrocarbon resources and are calculated to the year 2020. The difference between looking almost 40 years ahead and making an ultimate prediction adds little that is useful in the pattern of trends.

In making these estimates some assumptions have to be made and basically these are: (a) the price of oil will rise in real terms over the period to the year 2020, thus allowing a wider range of prospects to be considered than has been the case hitherto, (b) capital availability and political conditions will allow exploration and development to continue, and (c) oil recovery factors will rise from the present 30-35 per cent range to 40 per cent as recovery techniques improve.

To date discovered reserves total 1,115 billion barrels of oil, of which 635 billion remain to be produced. Discovered reserves of gas

Figure 1.11: Estimates of World Ultimately Recoverable Resources of Crude Oil from Conventional Sources

		x10⁹bbl.
1942	PRATT, WEEKS & STEBINGER	600
1946	DUCE	400
1946	POGUE	555
1948	WEEKS	610
1949	LEVORSEN	1,500
1949	WEEKS	1,010
1953	MacNAUGHTON	1,000
1956	HUBBERT	1,250
1958	WEEKS	1,500
1959	WEEKS	2,000
1965	HENDRICKS (U.S.G.S.)	2,480
1967	RYMAN (ESSO)	2,090
1968	SHELL	1,800
1968	WEEKS	3,550
1969	HUBBERT	1,350 – 2,100
1970	MOODY (MOBIL)	1,800
1971	WARMAN (BP)	1,200 – 2,000
1972	WARMAN (BP)	1,900
1972	MOODY & EMMERICH (MOBIL)	1,800 – 1,900
1972	BAUQUIS, BRASSEUR & MASSERON (IFP)	1,950
1973	SCHWEINFURTH (U.S.G.S)	2,964
1973	ALBERS (U.S.G.S.)	1,330 – 13,300
1973	LINDEN (INST. GAS TECHNOL.)	2,945
1974	BONILLAS (SOCAL)	2,000
1974	HOWITT (BP)	1,800
1975	FREZON (U.S.G.S)	1,220 – 12,200
1975	MOODY (MOBIL)	2,000
1977	WORLD ENERGY CONF. "CONSENSUS"*	2,265
1977	NELSON (SOCAL)	2,000
1978	DE BRUYNE (SHELL)	1,600
1978	KLEMME (WEEKS)	1,750
1978	NEHRING (RAND)	1,700 – 2,300
1979	NEHRING (RAND)	1,600 – 2,000
1979	HALBOUTY & MOODY	2,130
1979	MEYERHOFF	2,190
1979	ROORDA (SHELL OIL)	2,400
1980	WORLD ENERGY CONF.	2,595
1981	HALBOUTY	2,275
1981	STRICKLAND (CONOCO)	2,071
1982	NEHRING (RAND)	2,400
1983	MASTERS & ROOT (U.S.G.S.) & DIETZMAN (E.I.A)	1,722
1984	THIS PAPER: MARTIN (BP) (to year 2020)	1,685

*Average of the two-thirds middle range replies out of 29 estimates.

amount to 4,690 trillion cubic feet (TCF) of which about 3,460 TCF remain to be used (Figures 1.12 and 1.13).

Figure 1.12: World Oil Discoveries to 1 January 1983 and Estimated Future Discoveries to Year 2020

billion barrels

	CUMULATIVE PRODUCTION	REMAINING PROVEN & PROBABLE RECOVERABLE RESERVES	DISCOVERIES TO 1.1.83	BEST ESTIMATE OF FUTURE DISCOVERIES TO YEAR 2020*	BEST ESTIMATE OF TOTAL DISCOVERIES TO YEAR 2020
NON-COMMUNIST WORLD	395	570	965	410	1375
COMMUNIST BLOC	85	65	150	160	310
TOTAL	480	635	1115	570	1685

*INCLUDES ADDITIONAL RECOVERY FROM EXISTING DISCOVERIES

Figure 1.13: World Gas Discoveries to 1 January 1983 and Estimated Future Discoveries to Year 2020

trillion cubic ft

	CUMULATIVE PRODUCTION	REMAINING PROVEN & PROBABLE RECOVERABLE RESERVES	DISCOVERIES TO 1.1.83	BEST ESTIMATE OF FUTURE DISCOVERIES TO YEAR 2020*	BEST ESTIMATE OF TOTAL DISCOVERIES TO YEAR 2020
NON-COMMUNIST WORLD	1000	2230	3230	2150	5380
COMMUNIST BLOC	230	1230	1460	1000	2460
TOTAL	1230	3460	4690	3150	7840

*INCLUDES ADDITIONAL RECOVERY FROM EXISTING DISCOVERIES

By simple arithmetic, at present rates of consumption, this oil will last for 32 years and the gas for 57 years. This simple calculation assumes that all fields will produce at a constant rate throughout their lives. However, a typical production profile of any field usually shows a quick build-up to maximum production as the field is brought on stream, a plateau period of maximum production, followed by a drawn-out steady production decline as the field reserves are exhausted (Figure 1.14). A global resource picture would show the same pattern, comprising the cumulative production curves of the world's oil and gas fields. Clearly, as the global reserve base declines the maximum production that can be sustained will also decline. Thus if no new oil is found the present level of production would not be maintained for 30 years and then stop dead. In reality a steadily declining production regime would be observed over a much longer period. New discoveries added to the global reserve base will prolong both the period of plateau production and the decline curve. Forecasting the global plateau production has to take into account factors outside the scope of this paper, such as world demand and political and economic environments, in addition to estimates of hydrocarbons yet to be found. However, it is clear that considerable quantities of oil and gas can be produced well into the next century, albeit from a declining resource base.

Figure 1.14: Forties Field Production Profile

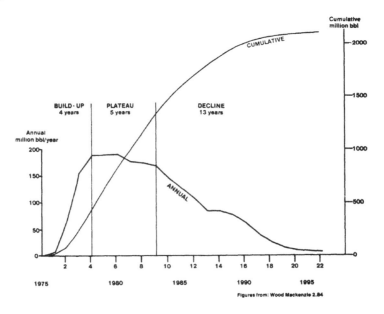

Figures from: Wood Mackenzie 2.84

Looking at the oil already discovered, it is seen to be distributed in a markedly skewed manner. To take a single oil province (in this case the Gulf of Suez) most of the oil occurs in a few large fields with the remainder spread over a long tail of much smaller fields (Figure 1.15). Not every oil province conforms to this pattern but the majority do.

Figure 1.15: Gulf of Suez Field Size Distribution

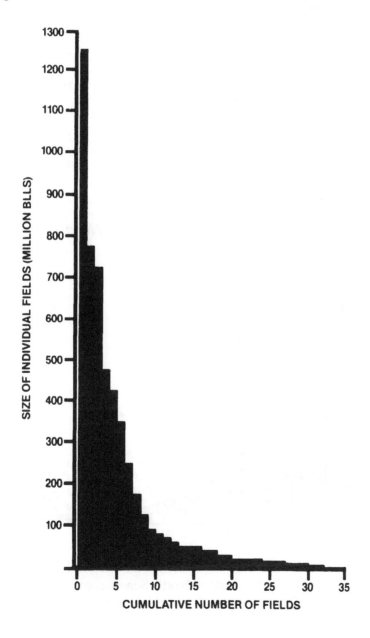

Figure 1.16: Size of World's Discovered Oil Fields

	NUMBER OF FIELDS	ESTIMATED RECOVERABLE RESERVES DISCOVERED	
		billion (x10⁹) bbl	% of total
4 largest fields:			
Ghawar, Saudi Arabia Greater Burgan, Kuwait Bolivar Coastal, Venezuela Safaniya/Khafji, Saudi Arabia/Neutral Zone	4	195	17
Fields with more than 10 billion bbl.	17	380	34
Fields with more than 0.5 billion bbl. (giant fields)	300	810	73
All fields	c.30,000	1115	100

Figure 1.17: Giant Petroleum Provinces of the World

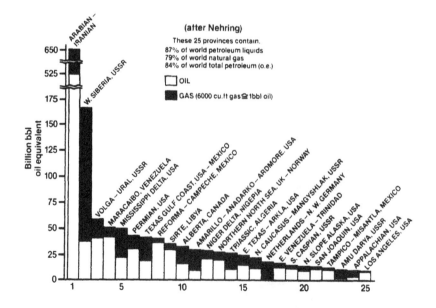

Expressed in a similar way 32 per cent of the 14.7 billion barrels of oil found in the United Kingdom North Sea is contained in three fields. If all the oil provinces in the world are considered, a similar global pattern emerges with 17 per cent of the world's oil in four fields and 73 per cent of the world's oil lying in less than 1 per cent of the designated fields (Figure 1.16). Thus the top 25 hydrocarbon provinces account for 87 per cent of the world's liquid petroleum discoveries and 79 per cent of the world's gas discoveries (Figure 1.17).

A practical consequence of this distribution is that the biggest fields tend to be the easiest to find and therefore are found early in the exploration of a province. Exploration of the United Kingdom North Sea exemplifies this with no giant field having been found since 1974 when the Magnus and Ninian fields were discovered (Figure 1.18).

Figure 1.18: UK North Sea Annual Oil Discoveries

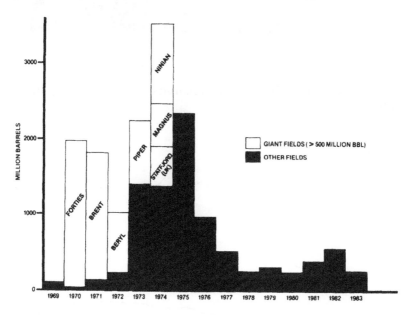

The enormous data base that is at the disposal of the industry has already been referred to and few sedimentary basins remain unexplored to some degree. It is therefore suggested that the same creaming off process seen in the exploration of each province has happened on a global scale. This took place especially in the 20-year period from 1948 to 1969 (Figure 1.19). Consequently, with few exceptions, most of the world's hydrocarbon provinces have been found. It follows that most of the remaining oil and gas to be found will be from provinces already discovered.

Figure 1.19: Contribution of Super Giants to World Oil Discoveries

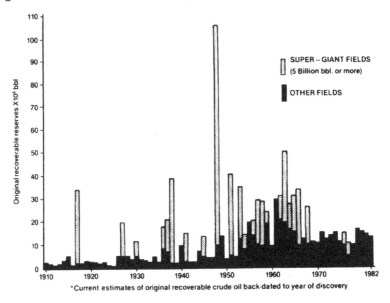

*Current estimates of original recoverable crude oil back-dated to year of discovery

Figure 1.20: Oil — Remaining Reserves and Annual Production, 1960-83

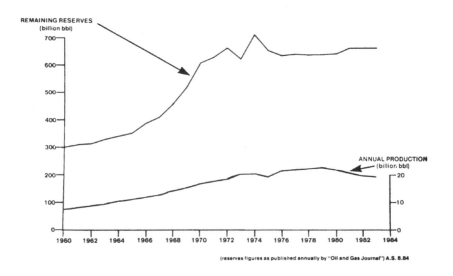

(reserves figures as published annually by "Oil and Gas Journal") A.S. 8.84

If this is so then henceforth the industry will be looking for ever decreasing volumes of future discoveries in generally smaller and smaller fields. The exploration for gas is not yet at the same stage but the eventual pattern must be similar. The pattern of world oil to date shows that during the last decade additions to reserves have been at a level of around 20 billion barrels per annum, counterbalancing annual production also of about 20 billion barrels (Figure 1.20).

During this period the discovery rate of new oil has not been as good as this because the figure includes additions and extensions to existing discoveries. These revisions arise from a variety of causes, most of which derive from a better understanding of a field when on production. Thus new oil over this period has probably averaged only 12 billion barrels annually. Figure 1.21 shows the estimate of reserves from known fields in 1971 and in 1981 with the reserves backdated to the year of discovery. The difference between the two curves to 1971 is the incremental oil from additions and extensions that have been made since 1971 to fields that were discovered before 1971. The importance of such oil is obvious and explains the much greater effort that the industry today is putting into reservoir and production engineering.

Figure 1.21: World Crude Oil — Remaining Reserves* and Production 1930-82

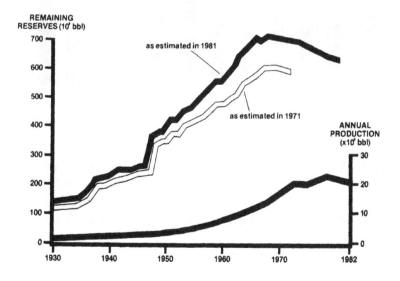

Note: *Current estimates of original reserves back-dated to year of field discovery.

During the period that new oil has been added at the 12 billion barrels per annum level, industry expenditure on exploration has more than trebled in real terms (Figure 1.22). Almost 130,000 exploration wells were drilled in the decade 1971-80 in the non-communist world (Figure 1.23). Even with this tremendous increase in effort there has been no significant improvement in the finding rate. This tends to confirm the creaming process and supports the conclusion, among others, that globally the industry is exploring the 'tail' of the world's oil resources.

Figure 1.22: Exploration Expenditure (converted to 1983 dollars)

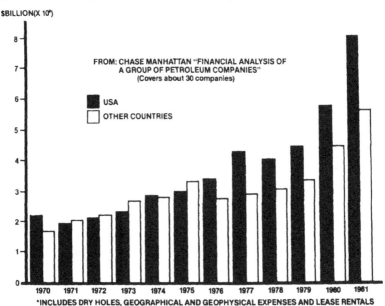

$BILLION(X 10^9)

FROM: CHASE MANHATTAN "FINANCIAL ANALYSIS OF A GROUP OF PETROLEUM COMPANIES" (Covers about 30 companies)

■ USA
☐ OTHER COUNTRIES

1970 1971 1972 1973 1974 1975 1976 1977 1978 1979 1980 1981

*INCLUDES DRY HOLES, GEOGRAPHICAL AND GEOPHYSICAL EXPENSES AND LEASE RENTALS

Thus, on the basis of the data available and the trends that can be established, British Petroleum concludes that oil discovered to date totals 1,115 billion barrels of which 480 have been produced. Another 570 billion remain to be discovered to the year 2020 giving a global resource of 1,685 billion barrels. The future discovery figure includes additions and extensions to existing discoveries (Figures 1.12 and 1.13).

Allowing for incremental oil, if new oil is estimated at 425 billion barrels, then the past decade's finding rate of 12 billion per annum would have to be sustained over the next 35 years. This consideration makes the estimate look on the high side of reality. It also carries the assumption that recovery factors in new discoveries will rise from the

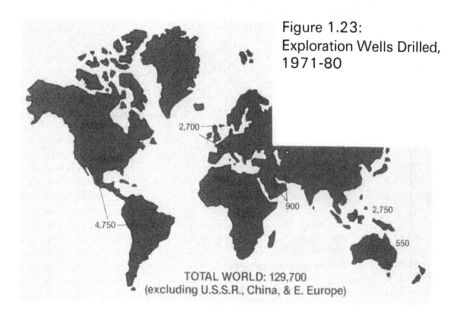

Figure 1.23:
Exploration Wells Drilled,
1971-80

TOTAL WORLD: 129,700
(excluding U.S.S.R., China, & E. Europe)

present 30-35 per cent to 40 per cent. This assumption does not recognise the fact that new fields yet to be found may well have a higher proportion of poorer reservoirs than in the past. Thus future average recovery factors could drop below those at present in spite of the considerable efforts being made in recovery technology. Such a trend in turn would reduce future expectations.

The situation for gas is brighter. To date 4,690 trillion cubic feet have been discovered, of which 1,230 TCF have been used. Future discoveries are estimated at 3,150 TCF giving a global gas resource of 7,840 TCF. Because of the nature of gas production there is less scope for this figure to be amended by improved recovery factors which already average 75 to 80 per cent.

In addition to these resource figures for oil and gas an additional total resource of perhaps some 200 billion barrels can be added for Natural Gas Liquids. The realisation of this resource will depend to a great extent on the development of natural gas production.

The distribution of oil discovered and future discoveries illustrates the dominance of the Middle East (Figure 1.24). Not only is this area dominant by virtue of its past discoveries (over 500 billion barrels) but future potential is large and may be even larger than estimated. For a variety of reasons it is difficult to obtain up-to-date critical data from three key countries in the region but the data that are available

Figure 1.24: World Crude Oil Production, Remaining Reserves and Future Discoveries to Year 2020

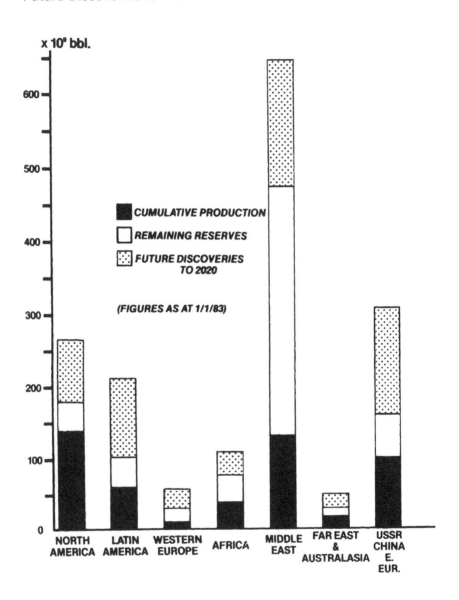

suggest that estimates of the future potential of Saudi Arabia, Iran and Iraq may be conservative.

Good quality data are also difficult to obtain from the communist countries, but the Soviet Union may be second to the Middle East with respect to future potential.

North America stands out as a mature exploration and production area. In view of the recent disappointing results in the US Arctic the future potential may be optimistically stated. Latin American potential is dominated by Mexico and Venezuela, while in Western Europe most future potential lies offshore the United Kingdom and Norway.

A somewhat different pattern is seen concerning gas. The Middle East is again a major source and the future potential may be understated as there is no doubt that the region is underexplored in relation to gas (Figure 1.25). The USSR stands out as the country with the largest gas potential both discovered and yet to be found while the North American figures illustrate the vast gas development that exists in the USA and Canada in relation to other producing countries.

Of future oil discoveries approximately 200 billion barrels (35 per cent) are expected to be found offshore and of the future discoveries of gas 1,200 TCF (35 per cent) may be expected to be found offshore. For sound geological reasons noted earlier these discoveries will be found peripheral to the continents and most will be made in waters less than 200 metres deep.

In conclusion, with two-thirds of the world's oil resource found, crude oil replacement rates have until now kept abreast of production. This situation does not seem likely to continue much longer if demand rises, despite the implication of our prediction that average annual new oil finding rates could continue close to current levels over the next three decades. By contrast although some 60 per cent of the world's gas may have been found only 15 per cent has been produced. This gives considerable scope for development where political and economic regimes allow.

Most new oil will be discovered within areas currently being explored and within known provinces. Field sizes are likely to decrease and hence the number of wells necessary to sustain finding rates will have to increase. More capital and more manpower will be needed to win the remaining resources. It will therefore be necessary for governments to recognise these factors if they wish for healthy and vigorous indigenous oil and gas industries.

Thus in the context of a finite and diminishing global resource any discovery, large or small, has a strategic value. The major problem, in

Figure 1.25: World Natural Gas Production, Remaining Reserves and Future Discoveries to Year 2020

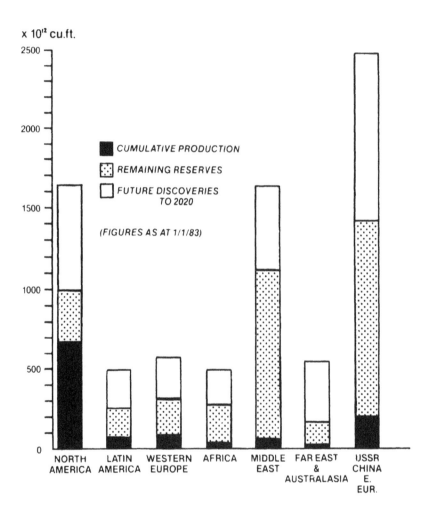

terms of global politics, lies in the fact that as oil resources diminish two regions, the Middle East and the USSR, will develop into an ever increasing dominance. The consequences of this will require all the skill that can be mustered if a sense of order and direction is to be maintained by industry and governments alike.

DISCUSSION

*Discussant: Professor J. Dewey, Head of Department of
Geological Sciences, University of Durham*

Mr Chairman, my competence, such as it is, is restricted to the area of geology, but perhaps I could just pick up a few points, some of which yield optimism and some pessimism. I would like, first, to thank John Martin for a brilliant talk on the geological framework for exploration. First, I should say that there have been two fundamental break-throughs in the last five years in the strictly geological aspects of oil exploration. One of those has been in the understanding of the physics of sedimentary basins. I think we now understand how sedimentary basins, these big depressions in which the oil and gas occur, originate — through what is called a stretching process. It is very clear that a fundamental stretching of the continental crust is taking place in many of the areas in which we find substantial reserves of oil and gas. The reason why, I think, many sedimentary basins exist in shallow water and onshore is that they exist in those areas where the continental crust has been very gently stretched. One of the great tragedies of oil exploration in the last few years has been that the continental margins, the places where continents have split and oceans have opened, have been found to be deficient in oil. We thought that this was going to be a major area for new oil and gas reserves. What has happened in these regions is that the rock has simply got too hot; one needs places like the mouths of the Mississippi and the Niger, where big deltas have added themselves to the edges of continents, to make these continental margins important.

The second area in which knowledge has recently advanced is with regard to producing oil in regions with unconventional rocks. The problem here, however, is how to find out that such regions do indeed have a potential for oil production. It is easy with hindsight to find the reasons why oil and gas occur in the places where they do, but it is not easy to get into the new frontier areas.

I would like, therefore, to ask John Martin the following question: to what extent does he think that the unconventional areas, like the red sandstone Newark and Connecticut basins of eastern North America, might become important in the future? Everyone 'knows' that red sandstone does not have oil and gas in it. There are both unconventional source rocks and unconventional reservoir rocks which have caused surprises. Are these areas of development significant, or are they trivial?

Dr Martin

I will split that up. When the unconventional basins, such as the Newark rift in North America with its thick red beds, are explored, there may be some surprises. I think, however, that most oil and gas in the future will be found in the oil provinces which have already been discovered. The oil provinces of the world basically are known, although there are certain ones which we know of and cannot get at: such as East Greenland and the Russian continental shelf.

I take Professor Dewey's point that we may, if we are lucky, come up with some surprises, but the 'unconventional' basins are in fact not very unconventional — or at least they are on the fringes of convention. We have now learnt a tremendous amount about source rocks. I touched very briefly on the generation of hydrocarbons; that field in the last decade has been a major field of advance in the oil exploration business. Our knowledge of the origin and generation of hydrocarbons has grown beyond belief in the last decade. The experience in the Middle East provides a classical example of the advance which has occurred. Despite the enormous hydrocarbon reserves, the chemists kept telling us that hydrocarbons could not be generated from limestone. All that is now understood and the chemists agree that oil can be generated from particular types of limestone. So I would say to Professor Dewey that if we look at new types of source rock maybe our field of knowledge will expand.

As for unconventional reservoir rocks, one runs into the same problem as one does with some of the unconventional sources (tar sands, oil shales and so on). So as to get poor reservoirs to work you need to put in a lot of energy — by way of steam, detergents or fire flooding — before you get anything out. The economics then all start to go wrong because you find that you are putting a barrel of oil in so as to get a barrel of oil out. If anyone asks me how much the price of oil needs to rise in order for production from oil shale to become economic, the answer is $US1 or $US5 more than the price of oil. We are a long way from making the unconventional reservoir commercial.

II INDUSTRIALISATION IN THE ARAB STATES OF THE GULF: A RUHR WITHOUT WATER

by Professor A.A. Kubursi
Department of Economics, McMaster University, Hamilton, Ontario, Canada

Introduction

Were oil supplies everlasting and the demand for oil strong and continuous, economic diversification or industrialisation would be without advantage for the member countries of the Gulf Co-operation Council (GCC) region. Instead, their governments would need only to ensure the distribution of oil revenues among the population. However, this is far from being the case. Oil reserves are finite and non-renewable, and the world demand for oil from the GCC region is not stable or continuous. Furthermore, at recent rates of utilisation, oil in the region will run out in the lifetime of the present generation (Bahrain, Qatar and Oman), its children (UAE), or its grandchildren (Kuwait and Saudi Arabia).

The states of the region, whether individually or collectively, face the striking realisation that, unless priorities and plans are set with care, the gestation period of economic development may be longer than the life of their hydrocarbon resources. They face the historical challenge of accumulating enough productive capital (both human and physical) in the non-oil sectors of their economies, and of raising productivity levels sufficiently in all sectors, to offset the drawing down of oil reserves. They are in a race against time.

If the race is to be won, there is no substitute for a general strategy — a co-ordinated set of general economic and social targets, designed to direct efforts and to bring about an outcome of the economic process different from that which would emerge spontaneously from the market system alone or from the continuation of historical trends. This strategy must of necessity embody a major industrial strategy.

Industrialisation, as a part of the development process, plays a number of major roles. First, it provides a means of diversifying the

42

economy to ensure balanced income-generation possibilities. It thereby plays a significant role in ensuring security of supply in an uncertain world. In a hostile environment there is no substitute for self reliance. Second, industrialisation plays a major role in training and even educating the labour force. A factory is as valuable as a school in upgrading skills, in instilling discipline, and in fostering collective and team work practices. It is a transformer of habits, attitudes, skills, and outlook. Third, industrialisation is a source of income: it raises the value-added component of domestic production and it increases the rent on local resources. Fourth, industry is a carrier of technology. It might make possible the development of products, machines, and processes that are better suited to the local circumstances. It lays in place an indigenous capability to control the environment and to adapt to it, and to adapt it to local needs and aspirations.

The Industrialisation Effort: A Perspective

Serious efforts at industrialisation in the GCC region are of recent origin. Before 1973 the price of oil was low, government revenues were low, and the oil industry had not been brought totally under national control. Nor had an infrastructure consistent with rapid industrialisation been fully established. The increase in oil revenues after October 1973, along with the increased ownership of the oil resources, provided an opportunity to put in place an infrastructure and to accumulate a surplus that would be capable of sustaining an industrial programme.

Current efforts at industrialisation in the region are characterised by three axes. The first axis includes industries based on oil and gas. It involves movement upstream and downstream in connection with the processing of oil and gas — including oil gathering schemes, refining, the liquefaction of natural gas, and the production of petrochemicals.

The second axis involves the processing of metals, especially the refining and smelting of aluminium, copper, and other metals where the energy requirements are extremely high and where, at the same time, energy feedstocks are required either as direct or indirect inputs into production.

The third axis involves movements offstream — to the development of industries that do not depend on oil as a feedstock. Here the developments have been far less ambitious, and have involved mostly the processing of consumer goods for the local domestic market.

These industries are largely concentrated in food processing, bakeries, confectionaries, printing and publishing, and other consumer-oriented products.

Oil Based Industries: Moving Downstream

The countries of the Gulf are no longer satisfied with their role as crude oil producers. They are moving to build a vertically integrated industrial structure covering transportation, processing, refining and marketing their oil. We will concentrate here on refining and processing, but this does not mean that the other aspects of this activity are any less important; they are simply not directly related to the issues addressed in this paper.

Petroleum Refining. Crude oil by itself does not have direct applications. Its full value is realised after it is processed into refined products for specific end uses. Furthermore, refining is a necessary first step for downstream development of fuel and non-fuel uses. In a series of processes, crude oil is converted into different fuels for energy uses as well as into lubricants, asphalt, waxes, gasoil and naphtha. The last two products are basically feed-stocks for the petrochemical industry.

There were less than 900 operational refineries in the world in 1980, with a combined capacity of about 80 million barrels per day. Refineries in the GCC region currently number 13, with a combined capacity of 1.5 million barrels per day, or about 1.9 per cent of the world capacity. There are a number of new refineries planned and some are already under construction. By 1986 these would raise the GCC capacity to 3.4 million barrels per day. With this increased refining capacity, the GCC countries, with an expected output of over 15 million barrels per day of crude, would be refining almost a quarter of their productions (See Table 2.1).

Refining in the GCC region started in Bahrain in 1937 with a 25,000 b/d complex, followed in 1949 by the 25,000 b/d Ahmadi plant in Kuwait, and then by Saudi Arabia's Ras Tanura refinery. These three refineries were, and still are, the largest refining centres in the Arab world. Currently, refining capacity in the region varies between 6,300 b/d (Umm Said) in Qatar to 500,000 b/d (Ras Tanura) in Saudi Arabia. The location, capacity, and type of each refinery in existence or planned are specified in Table 2.2.

The combined output of the GCC refineries will be more than sufficient to meet the expected domestic demand for refined products

Table 2.1: Oil Refining Capacity in the Arabian Gulf (Thousands of Barrels Per Calendar Day at Year End)

	Existing capacity 1981	Firm capacity 1986	Firm capacity increase 1981–6	Additional possible capacity[a] 1981–6	Firm + possible capacity increase 1981–6	Total firm + possible capacity 1986
All capacity						
UAE	15	195	180	550	730	745
Bahrain	250	250	–	–	–	250
Saudi Arabia	644	2,234	1,590	53	1,643	2,287
Oman	–	50	50	50	50	50
Qatar	11	61	50	–	50	61
Kuwait	594	594	–	106	106	700
Total	1,514	3,384	1,870	709	2,579	4,093
Estimated Export Capacity[b]						
UAE	–	100	100	550	650	650
Bahrain	225	200	(25)[c]	–	(25)	200
Saudi Arabia	300	1,365	1,065	53	1,118	1,418
Oman	–	–	–	–	–	–
Qatar	–	–	–	–	–	–
Kuwait	475	475	–	106	106	581
Total	1,000	2,140		709	1,849	2,849

Notes: a. 1981 on-stream + under construction + committed (for example, contract let as of Mid-January 1981).
b. Estimated on basis of announced intentions and domestic market growth expectations.
c. Figures in parentheses indicate decreases.
Source: Based on Field Missions and Reports of GOIC.

Table 2.2: Oil Refineries in the GCC Region, 1980

Country	Location	Capacity b/d	Type
Kuwait	Mina Abdallah	120,000	D
	Mina Saoud	50,000	D/R/B
	Shuaiba	180,000	D/H/R/C
	Mina Abdallah	120,000	D/H
	Mina Ahmadi	250,000	D/R/B
	Mina Ahmadi (under construction)	250,000	H/L
Saudi Arabia	Ras Tanura	500,000	D/R/B
	Jeddah	70,000	D/R/B/H/VIS
	Riyadh	20,000	D/H/VIS/R
	Ras Tanura (under construction)	25,000	R
	Jeddah (expansion)	170,000	D/VIS/R
	Al-Jubail (under construction)	120,000	D
	Yanbu (under construction)	250,000	D
	Al-Jubail (under construction)	250,000	D
	Riyadh (expansion)	120,000	D/R/H
	Rabgh (under construction)	350,000	D
Bahrain	Awali	250,000	D/C/R/VIS/B
Qatar	Umm Said	6,321	D/R
	Umm Said (planned)	50,000	D/R
UAE	Umm Al-Naar	15,000	D/R/H
	Ruwais	120,000	D/R/H
	Jebel Ali	200,000	D/R/H
Oman	(under construction)	50,000	—

Key: B = Bitumen, C = Cracking, D = Distillation, H = Hydrocracking, L = Lubricating Oil, R = Reforming, VIS = Visbreaking.

Source: GOIC, *Petrochemical Industries in the Arabian Gulf*, November 1980, p. 42.

and therefore will allow for exports. However, unit transport costs are much higher for refined petroleum than for crude oil. Thus, potential GCC exports will depend on transport capacity and the ability to effect reductions in crude oil exports. In 1980, the transport cost differentials between crude and refined oil per barrel were $1.44 to the US East Coast, $1.58 to Japan, $1.29 to North-West Europe, and $1.01 to Southern Europe. These differences in transport costs translate into refining cost differentials between the GCC and consuming countries of $1.30 with the US East Coast, $1.66 with North-West Europe, and $1.00 with Southern Europe. The differentials are not expected to fall before 1985. Thus, GCC countries are likely to face some difficulty in supplying refined products, except on a supply-demand balancing basis (filling gaps). Thus, a decision to expand refining capacity should be coupled with a decision to reduce exports of crude petroleum. Increased production should be directed to markets where competitive supplies are limited and capacity to transport the products on domestic ships should be expanded so as to counteract conference shipping rates which discriminate against processed products.

Natural Gas Liquefaction. The price of oil was relatively low before 1973, and as a result no capital investments were made to exploit the associated gas through liquefaction and export. After 1973, capital investments became economically feasible and many GCC countries moved to utilise their flared gases. Some started to liquefy methane and ethane, only to discover that this was costly and returned low net profits. Liquefaction at low temperatures (260°F below zero for methane, 129°F below zero for ethane), the use of refrigerated carriers, and the need to change liquid gas back to its gaseous state at the points of destination, proved too costly to net enough return on the large capital investment required. More recently, there has been a concentration on the liquefaction of propane, butane and natural gasoline.

Existing liquid natural gas production capacity in the GCC region is in the neighbourhood of 23,200 tons per year. Allowing for planned expansion, capacity in 1985 is expected to exceed 42,500 tons (see Table 2.3). Propane production is expected to be 15,000 tons per year, whereas butane and natural gasoline will each account for 11,200 tons per year. Saudi Arabia alone will produce more than 50 per cent of the expected total output. Kuwait and United Arab Emirates will each produce over 8,000 tons per year.

Petrochemicals. Hydrocarbons from petroleum and natural gas account for most of the chemicals produced today. Although it is difficult to devise a simple system classification to include all petrochemicals, it is customary now to use three broad categories to identify these products, namely, basic, intermediate and final products.

Table 2.3: Liquid Natural Gas Projects in the GCC Region

Country	Location	Present Status	Feedstock MCF/day	Products (thousand tons/year)					
				Ethane	Propane	Butane	Natural Gasoline	LNG	Total Liquid Gases
Kuwait	Mina Ahmadi	Operational	554	—	56	560	476	—	1,592
	Shuaiba	Operational	1,680	—	3,176	1,717	1,716	—	6,609
	Sub-total		2,234	—	3,732	2,277	2,192	—	8,201
Saudi Arabia	Ras Tanura	Operational	1,000	—	3,500	3,000	3,000	—	9,500
	Juaima	Under construction	—	1,423	2,851	2,190	1,914	—	8,378
	Yanbu	Under construction	3,000	1,262	2,376	1,200	990	—	5,828
	Sub-total			2,685	8,727	6,390	5,904	—	23,706
Bahrain	Manama	Operational	100	—	80	75	125	—	280
Qatar	Umm Said	Operational	360	—	336	270	270	—	876
	Umm Said	Under construction	340	—	270	157	113	—	540
	Sub-total		700	—	606	427	383	—	1,416
UAE	Das Island	Operational	550	—	650	420	220	2,300	3,590
	Al-Ruwais	Under construction	913	—	950	1,426	2,138	—	4,514
	Jebel Ali	Operational	140	—	311	222	244	—	777
	Sub-total		1,603	—	1,911	2,068	2,602	2,300	8,881
GCC Region	—	Operational	—	2,685	8,609	6,264	6,051	2,300	23,224
	—	Under construction	—	2,685	6,447	4,973	5,155	—	19,260
	Total		—	2,685	15,056	11,237	11,206	2,300	42,484

Note: MCF stands for millions of cubic feet.
Source: GOIC, *Petrochemical Industries in the Arabian Gulf*, November 1980, p. 40.

The main petrochemical basic products are the olefins (ethylene, propylene, butadiene), aromatics (benzene, toluene, xylenes) and methanol. Two primary processes are used in their production: steam cracking of naphtha for the olefins and catalytic reforming for the aromatics. A third process — steam reforming — is also used to synthesise ammonia and methanol. These products form the building blocks from which final petrochemical products are made. The processing chains from the basic to the final products are many and complex. However, a few chains dominate: ethylene and propylene are the main inputs in the making of plastics, aromatics in the making of synthetic fibres; butadiene and benzene in the production of rubbers, and methanol (converted into formaldehyde) in the manufacture of adhesives.

The economics of petrochemical production is also complex, involving complex technologies, large minimum efficient scales of production, high rates of product obsolescence, rising feedstock prices, and the dominance of transnational companies (TNCs) in the supply of petrochemical intermediates and performance products.

GCC countries are, however, in a privileged position when it comes to petrochemical products, given their abundant supplies of hydrocarbons, some of which are still virtually untapped (flared gas), and their abundant financial capital that could be productively invested in petrochemical production. Moreover, the low labour coefficients in petrochemical complexes match well the desire of GCC producers to reduce their reliance on foreign labour. In addition, in processing their own raw materials, GCC countries will increase the proportion of value added embodied in their resource-based products, diversify the market outlets for their products, and expose themselves to the industrial experience that is necessary for effective diversification of their overall economic structures.

The high rate of product obsolescence, the dominance of TNCs, and the high proportion of cost represented by feedstock call for a strategy of production in the GCC that concentrates initially on mature products whose markets can be captured by price undercutting. Thus, production of basic and simple intermediate products should precede the production of performance or end products. This does not argue for a total neglect of the end products; rather it argues for a gradual escalation of the complexity of the product structure in step with increasing experience. The historical record of this industry reveals a strong tendency for migration of production across geographical areas. Production started in the United States but migrated to Western Europe, then to Japan, and now to the Centrally Planned Economies. There is nothing to preclude its migration to what might be regarded as its 'natural abode' in the Arabian Gulf. The excess capacity of production in Europe and Japan is economically inefficient and vulnerable. The Arabian Gulf producers could use their strong leverage in world trade — they are large importers — and their position as major oil suppliers to obtain a substantial share of the market.

The high capital costs of petrochemical projects in the GCC region are balanced by the low variable costs of production. Besides, the capital costs themselves could be lessened by increasing the levels of domestic inputs in design, installation and management. The increased commitment of resources to build large-scale complexes increases the credibility and perceived seriousness of the GCC countries in the quest for a share of the world market.

There was a long time-lag between oil production and the development of petrochemical production in the GCC region. Low oil prices, and consequently limited capital, precluded the development of such a capital-intensive industry as petrochemicals. It was not until the late 1960s that petrochemicals were produced in the region. Fertilisers were first produced in Kuwait in 1966, and then at Dammam, in Saudi Arabia, in 1970. Since then, a large number of factories have been established in the region, producing urea and other types of fertilisers, and further development is under way. Table 2.4 presents figures relating to the existing and planned capacity for fertiliser production in the GCC region.

Qatar was the first GCC country to embark on the production of basic petrochemical products, with an ethylene complex in the industrial zone at Umm Said in 1974. The complex had a capacity of 280,000 tons per year of ethylene and 140,000 tons per year of LDPE. It was further expanded in 1980 to allow the production of 70,000 tons per year of HDPE.

There is currently no production of petrochemicals other than fertilisers in Kuwait. However, as Table 2.5 shows, a number of projects are contemplated. Similarly, the UAE is also planning a number of new projects, but there is none on line yet. Ethylene production is the main product planned by the Abu Dhabi National Oil Company. In Kuwait, however, a whole range of basic, intermediate and final products are being studied (for example, ethylene, HDPE, ethylene glycol, styrene, ortho-xylene and para-xylene).

A joint venture is under construction in Bahrain to produce

ammonia and methanol. Planned production of 1,000 tons per day of each is scheduled for 1984. Saudi Arabia, Bahrain and Kuwait are co-operating in this venture. There are no other petrochemical projects in Bahrain. Oman is currently studying the feasibility of producing ammonia and urea.

The largest regional petrochemical complexes are planned for Saudi Arabia, and two large industrial cities are under construction to accommodate them. The Saudi Arabia Basic Industrial Corporation (SABIC) is entrusted with operating these complexes, together with a number of TNCs. By 1986, the aggregate productive capacity is expected to reach 1.5 million tons per year of ethylene, 660,000 tons of LDPE, and 1.25 million tons of methanol, together with some small quantities of other products (see Table 2.5).

By the mid-1980s, the combined capacity of production of petrochemicals in the GCC countries will include the following: about 2.7 million tons per year of ethylene, or about 5.7 per cent of expected world production; 1.6 million tons per year of methanol, or 9.5 per cent of world production; 280,000 tons per year of ethanol, or 7 per cent of world production; 655,000 tons per year of ethylene glycol, or 12.1 per cent of world production; 635,000 tons per year of styrene or 5.4 per cent of world production; 800,000 tons per year of LDPE, or 5.1 per cent of world production; 400,000 tons per year of HDPE, or 4.9 per cent of world production; and 3.2 million tons per year of ammonia, or 6.8 per cent of world production (see Tables 2.4 and 2.5).

These shares are not high, and certainly far below the shares of proven reserves of gas and oil in the region and the corresponding production and export shares. The restriction of output to a narrow range of products is a wise short-term decision; broadening the base should be tied to the gaining of marketing experiences.

Equally important is the linking of investments abroad to GCC exports. This has already happened, but further and immediate attention is called for. There are today a number of projects. Kuwait, for example, owns 40 per cent of the Turkish Mediterranean Petrochemical Company. The Kuwaiti Fund is financing a urea and ammonia complex in Sri Lanka. Qatar owns 40 per cent of the French North Company which operates a petrochemical complex in France. Saudi Arabia has a petrochemical joint venture in Pakistan and another is contemplated with India.

The Non-Oil Manufacturing Structure in the GCC Region

It is pointless to address the issues of manufacturing within the

Table 2.4: Existing and Planned Fertiliser Industries in the GCC Region

Country	Location	Products	Capacity Thousand tons/year	Status
Kuwait Petrochemical Industries Corporation	Shuaiba	Ammonia	660	Operating since 1966
	Shuaiba	Urea	792	Operating since 1971
	Shuaiba	Ammonium sulfate	165	Operating since 1971
	Shuaiba	Ammonia	330	Planned
Saudi Arabia SAFCO	Dammam	Ammonia	180	Operating since 1970
	Dammam	Urea	300	Operating since 1970
SEMAD	Al-Jubail	Ammonia	330	Operational in 1983
	Al-Jubail	Urea	500	
	Al-Jubail	Ammonia	330	Under study
	Al-Jubail	Urea	500	
Bahrain Gulf Petrochemical Corporation (joint venture)	Satrat	Ammonia	330	Operational in 1984
Qatar QAPCO	Umm Said	Ammonia	297	Operating since 1973
	Umm Said	Urea	330	Operating since 1973
	Umm Said	Ammonia	297	Operating since 1979
	Umm Said	Urea	330	Operating since 1979
UAE ADNOC	Al-Ruwais	Ammonia	330	Operational in 1983
	Al-Ruwais	Urea	500	Operational in 1983

Oman				
Ministry of Oil and Mineral Resources	Sahar	Ammonia	200	Planned
		Urea	330	
GCC Region		Ammonia	1,434	Operating
		Urea	1,752	Operating
		Ammonia	990	Operational in 1983-4
		Urea	1,000	Operational in 1983-4
		Ammonia	860	Planned or under study
		Urea	830	Planned or under study
		Ammonia	3,284	Total
		Urea	3,582	Total
		Ammonium sulfate	165	Total

Source: GOIC, *Petrochemical Industries in the Arabian Gulf*, November 1980, p. 48.

Table 2.5: Existing and Planned Petrochemical Projects in the GCC Region

Country	Location	Products	Capacity Thousand tons/year	Status
Kuwait				
KPIC	Shuaiba	Ethylene	350	Planned
		HDPE	130	Planned
		Ethylene glycol	135	Planned
		Styrene	340	Planned
		Benzene	280	Planned
		Orth-xylene	60	Planned
		Para-xylene	86	Planned
Saudi Arabia				
(a) Saudi Arabia Petrochemical Co. (Shell Oil Co.)	Al-Jubail	Ethylene	656	Operational in 1985
		Ethylene dichloride	456	
		Styrene	295	
		Ethanol	281	
		Caustic soda	377	
(b) Saudi Yanbu Petrochemical Co. (Mobil Chemical Co.)	Yanbu	Ethylene	450	Operational in 1985
		LDPE	200	
		HDPE	90	
		Ethylene glycol	220	
(c) Al-Jubail Petrochemical Co. (Exxon Chemical Co.)	Al-Jubail	LDPE	260	Operational in 1985
(d) Saudi Methanol Co. (Japanese Consortium)	Al-Jubail	Methanol	600	Operational in 1983
(e) National Methanol Co. (Celanese-TEXAS Eastern)	Al-Jubail	Methanol	650	Operational in 1985

		Product	Capacity	Status
(f) Arabian Petrochemical Co. (Dow Chemical Co.)	Al-Jubail	Ethylene LDPE HDPE	500 70 110	Operational in 1985
(g) Eastern Petrochemical (Japanese Consortium)	Al-Jubail	LDPE Ethylene glycol	130 300	Operational in 1985
Bahrain Gulf Petrochemical Industries jointly with Kuwait and Saudi Arabia	Satrat	Methanol	330	Operational in 1984
Qatar QAPCO & CDF	Umm Said	Ethylene LDPE Propylene HDPE	280 140 5 70	Operational
UAE (ADNOC)	Al-Ruwais	Ethylene	450	Under consideration
GCC Region		Ethylene Ethylene dichloride Ethylene glycol HDPE LDPE Styrene Benzene Propylene Ortho-xylene Para-xylene Methanol	2,686 456 655 400 800 635 280 5 60 86 1,580	Total operational, operational in 1985, planned or under study

Source: Al-Wattari, *Oil Downstream* (Kuwait: OAPEC, 1980), pp. 98 and 99 and SABIC, *The Fourth Annual Report for 1400 A.H. (A.D. 1980)*, p. 22.

context of individual GCC countries. The question of size is particularly relevant in the context of manufacturing not only in terms of market size but also in terms of resource pools and human skills. The focus here is of necessity on the region as a whole — on what can be achieved and on the constraints and difficulties. The order of discussion is organised in terms of poles of production.

Resource Based Industrialisation. The strategy of basing industrial development on advanced stages of processing of natural resources is generally motivated by the desire to capture the high value-added component of such activities, to diversify production and exports, and to exploit such comparative advantages as may exist in the production of competitive commodities.

The successful involvement of GCC countries in the processing of raw materials and semi-finished goods will depend on a number of interrelated factors. Three such factors will be decisive: input availability; conditions of processing; and characteristics of output.

Input availability must be measured by comparative cost criteria. Raw materials and other complementary inputs are assessed in terms of their availability in sufficiently large quantities to make it possible to process them economically *in situ*. Whether they can be imported at advantageous prices, as an alternative to domestic supply, is another critical consideration (for example, bauxite from Australia).

The conditions of processing are determined by the technologies used in the processing activities, and here there are three main considerations. The first pertains to the extent to which economics of scale facilitate or impede the locating of productive capacity in the region, because of the abundance or lack of abundance either of the raw material itself or of other complementary inputs. The second relates to the range of technological choice available within the industry, and possibly to the availability of processing systems that are particularly suited to the conditions of the region. The third has to do with the development of new technologies or variants of existing ones, that may alter some of the circumstances militating against processing in the region.

The characteristics of output that are of special importance are those that determine the difficulties encountered in supplying end products to their markets, including transport and storage problems, tariff and non-tariff barriers, and other difficulties associated with marketing and distribution.

A recent study has indicated that non-ferrous metals, industrial chemicals, and petroleum refining are particularly low in labour intensity, when compared with other major production sectors. A study of investment potential in developing countries showed all resource-based industries except wood products to have capital-labour ratios of three to ten times the average for all industries combined, and labour coefficients 33 to 80 per cent below the average. Evidence such as this, although admittedly not conclusive, tends to suggest that this type of industrialisation is suitable for the GCC region.

Some recent changes in technologies offer significant opportunities for GCC countries. An example is the direct reduction of iron ore into sponge iron, using natural gas instead of coke. The sponge iron can be reduced to steel in electric arc furnaces, on a very small scale, using inputs of scrap of various qualities. The heavy use of natural gas and electricity, and the limited minimum efficient scale of the direct reduction method, provide a formidable comparative advantage to the GCC region, which has abundant gas and thermal electricity potential, and can import ore cheaply.

Smelting alumina into aluminium through electrolytic processes is again energy-intensive, as well as scale-efficient at low output levels, and capital-intensive. Moreover, the GCC region is advantageously located near Africa (particularly Guinea, which has over a third of the world reserves of bauxite). Similar advantages may be found in the smelting of copper and alloys (as is already the case in Oman).

Marketing opportunities in the Arab World, and in neighbouring Asian and African countries, are considerable. With a proper allocation of investment to activities in these regions, the GCC countries might bring into being a formidable procurement-distribution network, with benefit both to the GCC countries themselves and to the neighbouring regions.

Processing need not be confined to the region's own mineral deposits or other domestic resources. Raw materials or semi-finished goods may be imported for further domestic processing, and the products then used for home consumption or exported. This might be particularly desirable in the case of products that require intensive combinations of capital and energy and can be produced efficiently with relatively small-scale operations and limited water usage.

Four basic industries will be selected for examination here: iron and steel, aluminium, copper and cement. All of these activities are energy intensive and could be based on natural gas which is in abundance in the region. Their water requirements are moderate and their production could be coupled with desalination plants.

(1) Iron and Steel. Production of steel in the GCC region has not kept pace with consumption and the gap is expected to grow over the coming two decades. Whereas consumption exceeded 3.3 million tons, production in the region fell short by 0.7 million tons in 1978. Over the next two decades consumption is forecast to reach 17 million tons by 1995 whereas production is not expected to exceed 3 million tons.

Of the dozen or so combinations of processes for making iron and steel, the one which merits serious consideration by GCC member countries is the direct reduction of iron ore to make sponge iron followed by electric arc furnace treatment to produce finished steel. The direct reduction process to produce sponge iron and steel using natural gas has many advantages. These include operating simplicity, lower capital costs compared to blast furnace operations, suitability for small-scale operation and non-reliance on imported scrap to make steel (Saudi ores could be beneficiated and used too).

The case for locating direct reduction plants in the GCC member countries rests mainly on the availability of low cost energy — gas for the ore reduction process and relatively cheap power for an associated electric furnace steel plant. The price at which gas is made available to a new iron and steel venture is therefore a key to its profitability and future viability.

The question often arises as to whether production of iron and steel should be geared for domestic use or export. Given the large gap anticipated between production and consumption, this issue is not likely to be significant in the GCC region for some time to come.

The iron and steel industry does not operate in a vacuum and as such care must be exercised to co-ordinate the erection of capacity to produce these products in isolation of using feeder industries. Balanced growth requires a complex strategy that co-ordinates all the phases involved. In particular the following industries need to be considered in a specific and systematic manner to meet the requirements of iron and steel plants in the region as well as consuming industries:

(1) castings and forgings
(2) alloy steel plants to cater to the needs of engineering and manufacturing industries
(3) graphite electrodes plants
(4) basic refractories plants.

Castings and forgings are the main raw materials needed by the engineering industry. Hence their establishment should be encouraged and given high priority.

(2) Aluminium. Aluminium production is energy and capital intensive. With low cost energy, suitable geographical location, large investment funds, and low environment sensitivity, the GCC region is considered well placed for production of this commodity. Low cost electrical power will remain the key to economic production of this product and GCC member countries may therefore be able to compete by using their gas to generate the necessary power in gas turbines.

The primary aluminium industry, which comprises mainly smelters, is presently located in the GCC region in Bahrain and United Arab Emirates. The total capacity of both smelters in the region amounts to 255,000 tons (120,000 + 135,000).

Several other states are at the stage of planning new facilities among which are:

Bahrain (expansion) by	45,000 tons
Qatar	150,000 tons
United Arab Emirates	150,000 tons
	345,000 tons

In the event that all these plans are implemented, then total production capacity will approach 600,000 tons, which is in excess of the anticipated regional consumption level in 1990. Therefore the new plants have to be reviewed in terms of their access to world market and future price levels. Saudi Arabia had contemplated the construction of a smelter with 200,000 tons capacity. Recently it shelved the project preferring instead to become part owner of Bahrain's ALBA.

Among fabricated products, rolling is considered a highly capital intensive industry. Moreover rolling products represent the largest portion of consumption of aluminium in the region. These products are normally: plates of 6.45 mm thickness and above, sheets of 0.15–6.32 mm thickness, foils of less than 0.15 mm thickness and sections. Other fabricated products are processed through castings, extruding, forging and drawings.

Several processing units related to extruding and drawings exist in the region, but only recently a rolling mill with a 40,000-ton capacity has been agreed to by Gulf countries, as a joint venture enterprise, to be erected in Bahrain. It was to be commissioned in 1983/4. The product will mainly meet the local demand.

Apart from alumina, the other main materials required for production of aluminium are: cryolite, aluminium fluoride, electrodes or electrode materials (carbon and pitch) and petroleum coke, which materials represent more than 10 per cent of manufacturing costs. Therefore studies should be carried out in order to find the viability of producing aluminium fluoride, cryolite and petroleum coke in the region in sufficient quantities to feed the existing and planned smelters.

(3) Cement. This industry is perhaps the best suited for production in the region given that most of its raw material requirements are available within the region. Moreover, gas is an ideal input in the production of clinker and cement, and gas is abundantly available in the region. Nevertheless, until very recently the region imported large volumes of cement, but this was the result of a unique situation that is not expected to hold for long.

In the meantime, a large number of cement plants were constructed and now, except for Oman, every GCC state has at least one cement plant. By June 1982, the GCC *installed capacity* amounted to over 14 million tons and this is expected to rise to almost 24 million tons by the early 1990s. Should local demand moderate its growth, the region may be in a position to export its surplus to other neighbouring countries. Given the high transport cost of cement, it is not likely that much exports can be anticipated from the region and as such capacity extensions should be undertaken with special care.

The choice of technology lies between a wet or dry process. For most GCC countries, the dry process should be chosen because of its lower water requirements as well as lower energy consumption.

(4) Copper. The GCC region contains a large tonnage of poly metallic sulphides. The principal minerals are pyrite, chalcopyrite and sphalerite, which are, respectively sources of iron, copper, and zinc. Copper is actively mined currently at the Sohar region of Oman and is smelted into about 20,000 tons per year there; further processing of copper by electrolytic refining (20,000 tons per year) is scheduled to take place in the near future. Copper mining is potentially economic in Saudi Arabia too. The Jebel Saud deposit is

an example of a deposit that could be economically mined; it could produce from 1 to 1.3 million tons of ore per year, depending on the method of exploitation.

A second example is the Nuqrah area deposit in Saudi Arabia which could be economically exploited by underground mining for a period of up to twelve years at a rate of up to 140,000 tons of ore per year. The deposit is five to seven times richer, in terms of ore value, than other copper deposits in most developing countries.

The current practice of copper mining, smelting, and planned future refining in Oman has produced some experience in the domain of integrated copper production which will be useful in planning any further development in the GCC region.

Whereas moving downstream or upstream in the oil and gas sector represents exploiting vertically the comparative advantage of the region, developing the mineral resources of the region or processing further within the region imported ores represents exploiting horizontally the comparative advantage of the region in oil and gas, capital abundance and availability of raw materials. There are two added dimensions to this horizontal extension of comparative advantage — first, the potential use of local ores and secondly, utilising complementary inputs usually produced as by-products of oil and chemical refining in the region. As examples of the first dimension it may be possible to mention the iron ores in Wadi Sawawin, Jebel Idsas and Wadi Fatima in Saudi Arabia. On the other hand, petroleum coke and caustic soda are illustrative examples of the second dimension.

The region's abundant energy supplies, its prime geographic location and its sparsely populated areas qualify it to embark on a serious evaluation of major extensions and expansions in the direction of further processing local and imported minerals.

Food and Agricultural Processing. Food security considerations, raising the embodied domestic value added in local resources and encouraging the private sector to capture industrial opportunities provided by the larger GCC market combine to make food and agricultural processing a potentially desirable activity in the region.

Processing opportunities for traditional agricultural products, however, are fairly limited. The bulk of domestic production serves local needs and is often produced, processed, and consumed within a local market area. At this level, given the general lack of statistical information in the region, there is a considerable amount of uncounted activity. Data gathering procedures do not operate well at this low level, particularly if the exchange process has no records. Traditional cash crops, such as dates and citrus fruits, require little in the way of processing prior to sale, either domestically or on the export market. Thus, agricultural processing is based primarily on expanded production of vegetables, livestock, and other non-traditional crops, or on the processing of imported raw materials, such as cereals and semi-finished products. Two types of processing structures can therefore be distinguished. The first involves a forward linkage from domestic production, and depends for its growth on the expansion of local agricultural output, either crops or livestock. The second is oriented toward transforming raw materials purchased abroad into final products.

Although the agricultural processing industry has several general characteristics that would appear to make it an unlikely sector for major growth within the region, on balance there are still several net benefits. In many cases, primary agricultural inputs to the industry are highly perishable. This eliminates the possibility of importing the raw material for local processing. For these types of processing facilities, such as meat packing and vegetable canning, any plants would have to rely on local supplies. In order to produce at prices competitive with processors in other areas of the world, the local industry would need heavy subsidies or low raw product prices. If, however, raw product prices are low to the farmer, so that the costs of production exceed the returns, the output will not be produced and the industry will be unable to operate. Thus, the implication is that, unless farmers can profitably produce the product at a low price, the processing industry will require subsidisation or tariff barriers to inhibit foreign competition, at least initially until such time as the domestic industry is mature enough to compete on equal footing with foreign suppliers.

A second consideration is that most processing activities tend to be weight-reducing: the product loses weight during processing. Thus, waste is produced and discarded. This typically leads to processing plants locating close to the primary sources of raw agricultural product in order to take full advantage of reduced shipping costs. For the GCC states, processing plants that rely on imported raw materials (such as oil seed crushing plants) will be high-cost producers unless a relatively high value can be assigned to their by-products, and these are many and often substantial. Otherwise, all of the large shipping bills associated with transporting the raw material will have to be assigned to the cost of producing the desired products.

Ultimately, the factor that most limits expansion of agricultural processing is the high cost of water in the region. Traditional agricultural processing plants use high volumes of water in virtually every stage of processing. Where the costs of water are high, processing of food products is a high-cost activity.

All of these influences place severe limitations on the growth potential of the food processing sector, particularly as an export-oriented industry. Opportunities for expansion of the sector will arise primarily through import substitution. In this vein, Oman has recently completed a feed mill in Muscat to formulate feeds for livestock. This will reduce the need to import such feeds. To the extent that local agricultural production can be increased and made available, a small but viable processing sector could develop. This is most likely in the poultry processing and vegetable processing sectors. Recent advances in recycling technology have reduced the water requirements for food processing plants. Using advanced technology, a net surplus of water can be produced. Of course, the costs of this technology are high, but such plants may appear viable when account is taken of the price of importing the processed product. Similarly, industries based on imported raw materials may be viable operations within the region if their waste products are not excessive.

With the great increase in population in the region, considerable opportunity exists for the beverage industry. Since the production process consists of adding water to a concentrate prior to packaging, the transport costs of the raw materials are low. Furthermore, the final product sales price is relatively high and will more than cover the true value of the water.

To the extent that the region's population reaches a large enough size that processing plants can take advantage of economies of scale, there is opportunity for increased activity. However, the particular type of operation must be chosen carefully if costs are to be kept under control.

Expansion of fisheries is another activity with high potential in the region. A by-product of this activity is the large volume of by-catch. Approximately, 8,700 tons of by-catch were available in the region in 1979. The growing production of broilers and eggs in the region provides a major opportunity for the utilisation of this by-catch. Fish-meal can be used as a protein supplement in livestock feed. Expansion of existing feed milling facilities to produce feed using an indigenous product would reduce import costs and provide stimulus to local fisheries.

Current food and agricultural processing activity in the region is limited but data on this subject are particularly difficult to come by and to organise within a consistent framework. Consequently, the available material is presented on a country by country basis.

Bahrain possesses some food processing capacity but this would seem to be designed solely for domestic production and to rely primarily on imported raw materials. Data for Kuwait are available for 1977, in which year Kuwaiti authorities counted 346 bakeries, 16 confectionary producers, 14 producers of dairy products, 7 animal feed producers, and 4 bottling operations. Not surprisingly, bakeries dominate the sector in terms of numbers as they produce a highly perishable product which requires limited investment in capital or technology. Oman has developed fruit packing plants in Batinah and Salalah to take advantage of local production. In addition, there are new date storage facilities in Muscat. The country also has dairy facilities capable of producing 0.72 million litres of yogurt and 1.5 million litres of milk products. Flour milling capacity has recently been expanded and a new animal feed plant has been constructed. There are also the usual bakeries and confectionary operations found in all communities.

Qatar possesses minor meat packing and dairy operations, in addition to bakeries and other local supply facilities. Saudi Arabia has the most extensive set of processing facilities in the region.

Capital Goods and High Technology Products. Aside from natural resource-based industries and the other growth poles mentioned above, there are many industries which are likely to be viable candidates for co-operation among GCC member countries. One such area is in the field of heavy engineering industries which we refer to here as the capital goods pole. These industries are characterised by quite heavy capital investment, highly skilled manpower, and a long maturation period. Another outstanding characteristic is the existence of a large number of links between their output and that of other productive activities (forward and backward linkages). The linkages of these industries lend themselves also to split production whereby certain products produced in one country of the GCC can be used as inputs in other plants located in another GCC country.

A review of the structure of manufacturing output in the GCC member countries reveals that more complex and integrated activities in the engineering industries have only recently been given attention by some member states. The lack of financial resources, the limitation of the market at the country level, and the absence of a co-operative outlook among the member countries in the past may have inhibited the establishment of such industries.

With the exception of Saudi Arabia in the case of a limited number of industries, the GCC member countries individually will not be able to develop viable industries in this field because each member country, when operating alone, lacks one or more factors necessary for the development of viable and dynamic engineering industries. Thus it would appear that in the GCC countries collectively, the high level of demand for capital goods which has been created by their ambitious development programmes can serve to encourage the rapid expansion of the capital goods industry within the region. As an indication of magnitude of demand, we note that the region's import of engineering products increased from $US1,392 million in 1973 to $US13,420 million in 1978. During this period, the member countries spent an average of close to 14 per cent of the gross domestic product (GDP) on imports of such products. Present indications suggest that such a trend will continue for some time to come. Actually, the forecast for 1990 puts the amount for engineering products in the GCC region at $US22 billion. The region cannot afford but to develop a host of activities in this area to balance its production structure.

Conclusion

Pointing to the potentialities of a selective approach to industrialisation does not mean that we can simply forget about balance in the development process and functions. We cannot ignore either the technical input-output relations of production or the demand patterns of the ultimate consumers.

The process of and the planning for industrialisation must be holistic and comprehensive. Alternatives must be weighed against one another and complexes and networks must be considered simultaneously and together.

The end of the oil era is in sight and the gestation period of development of the region could extend beyond the life-span of hydrocarbon resources of the region. Selectivity, carefulness and co-operation are key functions for the success of the regional development effort.

DISCUSSION

Discussant: Mr R. Belgrave, Head of Joint Energy Policy Programme, Royal Institute of International Affairs, London

I wondered why I had been invited to act as the discussant for Dr Kubursi's very interesting and very sophisticated paper. I guess that it is maybe because I have something of a reputation as a Luddite. For those of you who are less familiar with English history, they were people who went out and broke up machinery during the Industrial Revolution in this country because they thought it was a bad thing. I personally feel that it is important not to regard industrialisation as an end in itself. There are aspects of it that we would have been better off without. You only have to go out into some of the small towns round here to see what I mean. So if I seem to be rather critical, and I guess that is my job, it is not that I think industrialisation should be confined to the OECD world, or to Europe, or to anything of that kind.

The thesis of Dr Kubursi's paper is that the oil is going to run out soon and that there must be a positive industrial strategy to put something in its place. I was reading the diaries of a cousin of mine, who was Adviser to the Amir of Bahrain in 1936. He writes in these diaries that an era of great prosperity was beginning for Bahrain now that oil had been discovered — provided it did not run out. His informants were telling him that perhaps he had ten years. We were given reasons earlier why the decline may be more slow than people have supposed and, of course, as the decline takes place the price, the real price, will go up. I would suggest that the region has a little bit more time than Dr Kubursi supposes.

Although there are those who say that economic development is best left to the market, and those who point to planned developments in other parts of the world which have proved ineffective, there is none the less an argument for a positive industrial strategy. There is an enormous amount of leeway which has to be made up and I think there has to be a strategy. What an industrial strategy cannot overcome is the forces of the international market outside. That, I think, is the real core of the comment which I wish to make.

If you take the case of oil refining, the terms of trade have turned unluckily against the Gulf countries in the ten years in which refining has been developed there. Ten years ago foreign companies were falling over each other to enter into deals with the Gulf countries for industrialisation in return for access to crude oil. They are less interested in that now than they were, but it may change again. Equally, with OPEC accounting for a falling proportion of global oil production, it will become more difficult for OPEC to maintain a stable price.

One further point about the oil running out is that the gas is there in even greater quantities, as we have heard from Dr Martin. This provides the greatest natural competitive advantage for the area, particularly in terms of the route into chemicals. There is, however, a problem here. This morning Sheikh Nasser quoted Mr von Wachen of Shell as saying that he hoped artificial barriers would not be introduced to hinder the movement of chemical products. Of course, Shell will hope that, but Shell do not always get it all the way they want.

Turning now to metals. Of course there is a great opportunity for industry based on local raw materials. Cheap and plentiful energy supplies can make such an operation highly economic. Technology, however, can change and the industrial processes which require much energy today may no longer do so in the future. The operation of steel foundries in the Gulf would then no longer be so economic.

The characteristic of the Ruhr was that it had a great concentration of people, a ready-made market on its doorstep, and it had water. I was a little surprised that water was not mentioned as part of the industrialisation of the Arab Gulf. The production of desalinated water now seems, in itself, to be a very important industrial activity and one which could make it possible to reverse the decline in local agriculture — leading to the actual production, not just processing, of local food.

I would be very interested to hear from the people in this Symposium about the extent to which the Gulf Co-operation Council is able to organise the degree of specialisation among its members. We were given one example of Saudi Arabia taking a shareholding in the aluminium plant in Bahrain and I would think it would be very interesting to hear if there are others — because that seems to me the key to providing a big enough market for some of these industrial developments.

Finally, alternatives offstream. I would like to remind you that there is an alternative to offstream industrialisation, namely to concentrate on offstream developments which are non-industrial. Bahrain, and to some extent Kuwait, has been very successful in developing banking services. One should also bear in mind the importance of educational development. In this country the Scots have been extraordinarily successful at educating people despite having few indigenous resources.

Dr Kubursi

I would like to make three points in response to Mr Belgrave's comments. First, industrialisation is indeed not separable from the total development process: it is an integral part of development. If I am arguing that industrialisation is a way to diversify the economy, that does not mean that other aspects of the development process should be neglected. On the contrary, industrialisation must be considered within the context of overall development and that includes the many different sectors of human life.

Second, I am very cognisant of the fact that technology does change — and changes very rapidly. Changes have recently occurred in the production of petrochemicals: multinational corporations are now attempting to produce ethylene directly from methanol, without passing through ethane at the intermediate stage. There is one major consideration here which needs to be emphasised. The countries that are able to adjust best to technological change are those that already have the technology. This provides a reason for developing countries to move into even the simplest industries, because once you have the industry established you can move into more advanced forms of technology. Ultimately industry is not machines and industrialists, it is basically skills. These cannot be learnt from books but have to be learnt in practice. This is the most famous economic dictum of industrialisation and I think there is no substitute for it.

Third, the question of water. You are quite right that whereas oil is the major propeller of growth in the Gulf area, water is the major constraint. This is one of the things which the GCC has really been very serious about. The GCC has taken stock of the water balances and has found that water is in fact in surplus to needs. The problem, however, is one of distribution: you have to move it from places where it exists in surplus to places where it is in deficit. The whole area is sitting on a common aquifer. The states have a common reservoir, where the use by one country affects the use by another, and they really do need to co-ordinate this.

Chairman

As I understand free markets, they are based on two elements: needs and the ability to pay. I can see that world-wide there exists substantial need for the products which would emerge from a developed Gulf petrochemical industry, but I am not so sure that I can see the ability to pay. If you were to put into money terms the projected petrochemical production of Europe, North America and the Gulf states, is there enough money available in the countries that need to buy to promote the sale?

Dr Kubursi

If we consider the indigenous market in the Gulf, then there is an abundant amount of money: the area has a very high *per capita* income. Domestic demand, however, cannot be the only component and one has to think about exports. Here one has to be very careful. Although I understand and appreciate the premises and rationale of the Saudi strategy, which is to enter joint ventures with the multinationals so as to ensure that the latter find the markets for Saudi petrochemicals in the West, I prefer the Kuwaiti strategy. The Kuwaitis have been investing in some downstream industries in developing countries, with a view to those industries constituting a committed market for Kuwait's petrochemical products. They have done this with the Turkish Mediterranean Company and with two plants in India and Pakistan.

The most important thing for the Arab world is economic depth. The wider Arab world will not be able to purchase the products of the Gulf states unless these states invest there in a co-ordinated manner. One has to create the purchasing power in the Arab world; joint ventures between Gulf states and other Arab states need to be established so as to create this purchasing power. The Gulf states could invest in agricultural processing in Sudan, in cosmetics in Syria and Lebanon, in fertilisers in Tunisia, etc. There are really ample opportunities. Currently the Arab non-oil producing countries have only limited purchasing power, but this could be augmented to the benefit of all if a co-ordinated system of investment could be implemented by the oil producing states.

Question

The issue as to whether Gulf petrochemicals will be allowed access into Western markets should perhaps be directed to Mr Wiggins. I wish to ask Mr Wiggins, therefore, whether the British government will pursue a protectionist policy in keeping Gulf petrochemicals out. As Britain already has some problems with its petrochemical industry, why does the government not seek to restructure that industry so as to leave the market open for Gulf exports? This is how the majority of people in the Arab world would understand the word 'co-operation'.

Mr Wiggins

This point should strictly, I suppose, be answered by the European Commission, in so far as the British government is not any longer directly responsible for tariff policy. My understanding, however, is that such barriers as there are to the import of materials of this kind into the Community are pretty small and could quite readily be overcome by small price variations on the part of the producers. I think it is much too soon to talk about some sort of conspiracy to refuse to admit these products. It is also my impression that the international companies are themselves co-operating to bring these products in, and that in north-western Europe they have already restructured their petrochemical industry substantially — there have been closures of petrochemical plants on quite a large scale.

One does need to look again at the former strategy, which was for us to devote considerable resources to the very large-scale production of petrochemicals. This may not have paid sufficient regard to the impact of such investment on the petrochemical industry worldwide. It may in the long run be better and more satisfactory to develop an integrated industrial capacity in the Arab world.

Monsieur Michaux

I would like to comment briefly on what Mr Wiggins has said concerning the responsibility of the European Community for commercial matters. On the specific question of Gulf export of petrochemicals and oil-refined products, there are now some positive signs which have recently emerged after an official visit by the GCC officials to the European Commission. We hope that real negotiations on this matter will start within the next few months. On our side, at least, we are very optimistic about the results of these negotiations.

Sir David Roberts

My experience in the Gulf has been that where the level of economic activity has been raised and diversified from oil production, the new industries do not employ local people. They nearly always employ people from outside the Gulf — and perhaps outside the Arab world. Does this not in the long run pose a social and perhaps a political problem for the area, unless the expansion and diversification of economic activity is accompanied by the development of trained manpower?

Dr Kubursi

I very much agree with Sir David Roberts. Ultimately development is only meaningful when the people partake and participate in every single aspect of it. At present participation is not as widespread as is desirable; I believe we will see major changes in this respect. You cannot develop without bringing in local people.

Mr Wiggins

Is it a question of changing the habits of your culture?

Dr Kubursi

No, I would not accept that. There is no problem with culture. It is a matter of circumstances. If you have people who lack skills and education, it is difficult for them to participate in production. I do not think that the people in the area are culturally against industry or against work. The circumstances have been such that Gulf governments have had considerable sums of money at their disposal and little to spend it on. They can distribute this money by giving people jobs in the public sector. There are therefore people in public sector jobs who have no real work to do — because they do not have the skills and education to do useful work.

There are three aspects to look at in solving this problem. First, we should lay emphasis on types of development which are not labour-intensive. Now that the main infrastructure is laid down there is in any case no longer so great a demand for labour. Second, the people of the Gulf must really engage in productive work; income must be related to production. Third, in my view the Palestinians and other Arabs working in the Gulf should not be seen as expatriates. They should be deemed to be local people. You cannot develop the Gulf region with the indigenous people alone.

Susannah Tarbush

I wish to change the subject a little. You attach great importance in your offstream strategy, Dr Kubursi, to agriculture. Many people, however, are very worried about the way in which agriculture is developing in the Gulf: precious water resources are being mined, water tables are dropping, and agriculture is being encouraged by an enormous programme of subsidies — such that wheat is being produced at five or six times world prices. Do you think the current policy is on the right footing, and what agricultural strategy would you recommend for the next few years?

Dr Kubursi

As I said in my paper, the Gulf states have to make sure that they do not produce goods which use up water and are in fact of less value than the water they use. Water has to be valued by economic scarcity values. None the less, there is tremendous potential in certain areas. In one of the reports I refer to, it is stated that there are 22 products from whose processing more water is gained than was put in during the production process. It would be wrong to approach food security by means of seeking to produce every agricultural good which the area requires. Food security may be best served by a variety of different strategies; one of which is to invest in other Arab countries' agriculture.

Chairman

One final comment. Speaking as someone who has been deeply involved in the conservation movement in Europe, it seems to me important that the pattern of development is not such that people come to find the price too high once they achieve development.

III SCENARIO PLANNING IN THE CONTEXT OF INTERNATIONAL ENERGY DEVELOPMENT

by Mr G.S. Galer
Senior Consultant in Group Planning Co-ordination,
Shell International Petroleum Company Ltd, London

Planning and Forecasting

The methods of strategic planning used by many large companies, and by governments and government agencies, were called into question by the turbulent events of the 1970s and early 1980s.

They were based on the use of forecasts, of such items as sales, prices, production levels, costs, and other elements having important consequences for the outcome of business decisions. In turn, forecasts usually focused on a 'most likely' view of the future, which was generally a compromise between optimistic and pessimistic views.

In a relatively stable and growing world economy this approach was defensible, partly because in such a world the range of credible forecasts was necessarily quite narrow, but also because investment plans which turned out to be based on optimistic forecasts could usually be accommodated through subsequent market growth. However, the 1970s brought severe turbulence and, as its aftermath, slower and more variable rates of economic growth. Since that time dramatic price changes, volatility in exchange rates and variable inflation have become part of everyday business life.

Under these circumstances even the most sophisticated forecasters have had difficulty in producing accurate results. Examples of poor forecasting abound (Figure 3.1) and, while some of the choicest examples are to be found in the energy industries — past forecasts of coal demand or nuclear electricity production, for example — energy forecasters by no means hold a monopoly on inaccuracy.

Unfortunately, forecasts are normally developed at the request of decision makers, and in many cases, major investment decisions have been based on them. Clearly, forecasts made in the present business environment can be not only misleading, but dangerously expensive.

Figure 3.1: Estimates of Non-Communist World Oil Demand

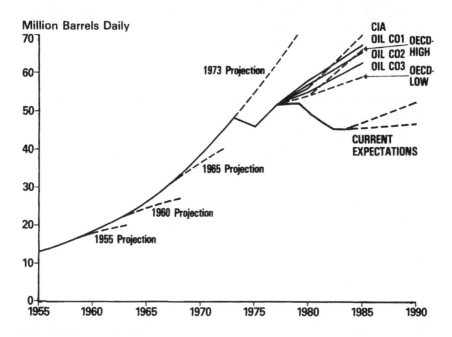

Uncertainty and Scenarios

While all may agree that, in principle, it is a potentially expensive 'intellectual swindle' to base business plans on forecasts of the single-line type described, the fact remains that strategic decisions have somehow to be made, and this is an environment where, as far as the oil and gas industries are concerned, investment lead times are long and tens or even hundreds of millions of dollars may be associated with a single decision.

Our response in Shell to this dilemma has been to develop methods of planning in which 'forecasts' are replaced by 'scenarios'. Scenarios are sets of credible, internally consistent but fundamentally different alternatives that portray future business environments. They are intended to challenge decision-makers and to alert them to the uncertainties against which they will, have to take decisions. Scenarios also help to test objectives and strategies. Although they invariably contain numerical data, they are intended to provide concepts and descriptions rather than detailed quantification. Scenarios should not be seen as alternative forecasts but rather as indicators of the interaction of key forces pointing the way to potential opportunities and threats.

Since scenarios attempt to increase our understanding of uncertainty, a basic step in the analysis is to identify those aspects of the future which are in fact highly uncertain, and to distinguish them from those which are largely 'predetermined'.

Predetermined Elements

These are events that have already taken place, or developments 'in the pipeline' whose consequences are likely to emerge under almost any future scenario. It is often possible to look at such things as economic structure, the growth potential of national or regional economies or political and legislative trends in this way. Similarly, some events can be excluded because they have not yet begun to happen, or because their impact would be too limited within a given timescale. For example, the discovery and development of a large new oil province, or a significant change in the composition of vehicle fleets, would fall into this category if one were considering the next five years.

Uncertainties

Typical examples of uncertainties which could seriously, if sometimes indirectly, affect decisions in the oil and gas industries are the pattern of technological innovation and its impact on various industries; changing lifestyles and attitudes; instability and socio-political pressures in oil-producing areas; radically altered structures and competitive pressures within the oil business. Then there are questions: in the OECD countries, what lessons are likely to be learned from the current period of stagnation and instability? Which countries will be able to 'restructure', at what cost and how quickly? Among less-developed countries (LDCs), what will be the future pattern of development, and what are its implications, in terms particularly of energy consumption and supply, for different countries and regions?

By combining creative imagination with rigorous analysis in exploring the interaction of these factors, attention can be focused on major uncertainties that could be relevant to current decisions. Internally consistent, qualitative scenarios are then developed to describe a credible range of alternative futures. The emphasis is on increased understanding of the potential for change: quantification of the scenarios is used mainly to establish their feasibility and to illustrate some of their implications.

Building Blocks

A competent scenario analysis will need to be built up from many carefully prepared components. Such 'building blocks' will include studies of economic growth prospects, energy conservation, inter-fuel competition and diverse other subjects.

One building block we have found useful in recent years has been called the 'oil tightrope' (Figure 3.2). Study of the outlook for oil demand and the prospects for supply from OPEC and non-OPEC countries has defined two bands of demand on OPEC, one above which conditions for rapid price escalation would be present and another below which OPEC cohesion would be seriously challenged, with resulting downward pressures on price.

Figure 3.2: The Oil Tightrope

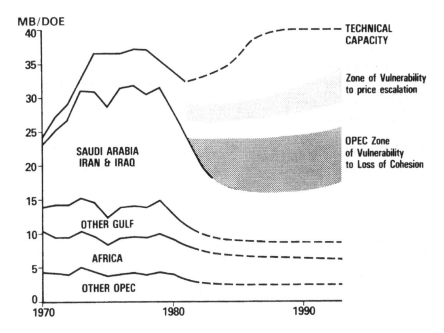

While OPEC has at times during 1982/3 shown signs of falling off the 'downward' side of this tightrope, it is by no means clear that this is going to continue to be the case during the later 1980s and 1990s. The tightrope analysis gives us a tool for studying the link between demand growth (itself scenarically dependent) and both the level and stability of oil prices.

Some Scenario Examples

In the *medium term* (the next five years) the scope for substantial change in the business environment for the oil industry is clearly more limited than over the long term (20 years or more). The medium-term uncertainties relevant to our business include the economic outlook, the continuing effect on consumers' demand of earlier energy price increases, changes in oil prices, instability in the Middle East and the whole question of OPEC oil pricing and production policy.

It could be said that the recent supply surplus of oil has been essentially a consequence of the 1973 price shock, following which new oil supplies were developed in the North Sea, Mexico, the USSR and the USA. As these sources began to reach peak production, demand for oil reacted to the 1979 price shock and fell steadily until early 1983. The trend of oil demand began to rise again in 1983 (although, for the world excluding communist areas, 1983 demand was still 1.7 per cent below that of 1982) and by the late 1980s the supply and demand picture could reverse again, if rising demand for oil once again interacts with less responsive supply.

In the *long term* we have three 'framework' scenarios for the world economy, each of which describes an evolution of geopolitical and economic events which will have practical consequences for the energy industries.

Restructured Growth. In which there is a dynamic response to current socio-economic problems, generating a new consensus for restructuring in social, political and industrial terms. There is a continuing decline within advanced economies in energy and oil demand per unit of GDP and steady growth in alternative supplies. The crude oil market is managed in such a way that relative stability is sustained. Real wage restraint permits recovery in corporate profitability and hence in investment, and market forces operate reasonably freely. New industries based on new technologies are a major impetus for growth.

World of Internal Contradictions. The 'business as usual' case sustained by a conventional economic recovery from the recession. There is a cyclical long-term growth but little attempt to tackle structural problems. Continuing uncertainty means a weak investment climate and there is widespread protectionism with conflicts over international trade. Energy conservation continues at moderate levels and there are continuing doubts about investments in new alternatives.

The potential exists for aggressive price leadership in the oil market and while prices are less stable, they remain at a generally higher level.

Harder Times. In which continued socio-economic problems further delay recovery from the recession, particularly in Europe. There is low growth with little industrial restructuring. High levels of conflict and instability continue. Energy conservation continues at a moderate level but there is little or no investment in alternatives. In the oil market, oil prices fall and the crude oil market begins to acquire the volatile characteristics of other 'commodity' markets.

The latter two scenarios do not describe a particular stable or comfortable route into the future and the first provokes the question, at least in some countries, 'how do we get there from here?' However all three contain elements which we believe are important in achieving understanding of the future for the oil and gas business. The scope for change over a 20-year period is enormous. What must be recognised is that all change produces opportunities and that these may be very different from those suggested by the present environment.

Energy Demand

Quantification of the scenarios gives some indication of the potential for changes in energy and oil demand over the next 20 years.

The energy and oil intensity of GDP in the aggregate of all countries outside communist areas has fallen substantially since 1973 (Figure 3.3). OECD countries are now seen as largely post-growth in energy consumption, with quite sharp reductions in primary energy use per unit of GDP over recent years. However, further reduction in future would vary markedly between scenarios and regions, depending mainly on the nature of government policies and on improvements in end use efficiencies. Total energy demand is expected to grow under all scenarios but oil demand, which peaked in 1979 at 42 million barrels/day (mb/d), had already fallen dramatically to 34½ mb/d in 1982 and 33½ mb/d in 1983. Oil demand may rise somewhat again when economic growth is favourable but a further fall in demand under 'Harder Times' conditions is quite possible.

In the developing countries, energy requirements will grow substantially over the next 20 years driven by continuing population

Figure 3.3: WOCA Energy and Oil Intensity

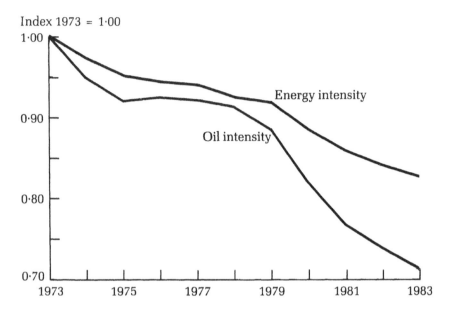

growth, urbanisation and industrialisation. Overall energy demand estimates are highly uncertain and depend on how fast individual economies grow and on the development pattern adopted. However, oil demand in these countries is expected to grow under almost any scenario. Substantial hydro-power resources are also being developed, and biomass could become a significant energy source in some tropical less developed countries.

Energy Supply

The sharp reduction in oil demand in recent years has postponed the previously expected decline in production. Even if oil demand were to reach 60 mb/d by the year 2000 in the world outside communist areas, production could be maintained at that level for some years. Conventional oil supplies will be maintained by several factors including further successes in exploration and production, enhanced oil recovery methods and higher conversion in refineries. Other conventional energy forms — hydro, coal, gas and nuclear — have emerged as much more serious competitors to oil but current oil prices have switched investment away from non-conventional alternatives, such as tar sands. Investment is unlikely to return until the cost of alternative energy sources is competitive with oil, which implies a considerably higher oil price. There still remain, however, opportunities for small local alternative energy projects where the scale does not present too great a risk.

Conclusion

Scenario planning in Shell is not a highly formalised activity, nor is it universally practised throughout the Royal Dutch/Shell Group, though it has gained wide acceptance in recent years at senior decision-making levels. Where it has been employed, however, it has helped us to learn more effectively, and to cope better with the uncertainties faced by a large, capital-intensive business in a highly volatile and unpredictable world.

DISCUSSION

Discussant: Dr F. Al-Chalabi, Deputy Secretary General, Acting for the Secretary General, OPEC, Vienna

It is obvious from the presentation that we are living in a world where uncertainties are growing, whether in the area of energy planning or in the area of economic growth. It is also obvious that with this increasing uncertainty, there is a need for more international co-operation, in order to reduce the degree of uncertainty. The previous forecasts about world energy demand and the world demand for OPEC oil have proved disastrous: the impact which they have had on the policy-making of companies and producing countries has been highly negative. The effects of erroneous forecasts on the producing countries have been far-reaching, distorting their economic development, their financial equilibrium and their pricing and production policies.

If you look back to what was said about world energy balances some four to five years ago, you will find that the world and all of the companies, institutions and governments were envisaging an energy shortage, placing world demand for OPEC oil well beyond OPEC's capacity. Forecasts made between 1976 and 1978 envisaged a world demand for OPEC oil in the range of 40 to 45 million barrels per day by the early 1980s, versus an actual OPEC capacity not in excess of 35 million barrels per day. What did that mean at that time? It meant that at that time, in order to cope with the envisaged shortage, prices had to shoot up and had to impose a dampening effect on the increasing world demand for OPEC oil, just to avoid an energy shortage. Now, after four to five years in which certain important developments have taken place in prices and production, the world is looking at OPEC oil just as a reduced residue in a world energy situation characterised by abundance or surplus. OPEC is now producing only about half its capacity and the situation of the 1970s has been drastically reversed. I believe that errors of this kind are harmful not only to the OPEC countries but to international economic development as a whole. There is, therefore, a need for some better form of co-operation on the international level in order to reach a better assessment of world energy balances. We could then avoid wasteful investments and achieve a better equilibrium in the world energy situation.

We have seen that in certain situations there appears now to be a growth in elementary demand for oil. The question which we must now face is: who is going to share in the resultant increased production? OPEC countries, I believe, should have an adequate share in this increased production, because OPEC has seen its share decreasing all the time, and this decrease in the OPEC share has greatly affected the economic development of OPEC members. OPEC cannot go on having a very small share in the world energy balance because the effect of that would be to create some internal forces in OPEC which may lead to price shocks in the future. I believe that it is in the interests of the international community (and OPEC is just a part of this) to achieve greater stability in the price of oil; that can only be achieved through greater co-operation. It is in this way that we can avoid the developments that took place in 1979/80, which proved very harmful to the world energy situation and to the world economy. We need also to secure at least a minimum of stability for the oil income of the oil producing countries. Better planning is the edict and this can be brought about only through reducing uncertainties and through more co-operation among the various partners of the energy trade.

Question

I can see the advantages of scenario planning from an educational point of view (that is, for the management), but I am not convinced that its practical effect is different from traditional forecasting. At some point a decision has to be taken whether or not a refinery is going to be built or whether an oil field is going to be developed. At that point the scenario has to be turned into a more traditional forecast. Apart from educational elements, then, what are the advantages of the scenario approach?

Mr Galer

Putting forward different scenarios helps to make clear the whole background relevant to coherent decision-making. Possible developments in strategic innovation or investment can be tested against different scenarios, to see what effects particular decisions would have under varying conditions. If the outcome of a particular move is the same in all the scenarios, then we have a robust decision. If the outcome would not be positive under one or other of the scenarios, the company would have to make a clear evaluation of the likelihood of the different scenarios coming into existence and therefore of the risks inherent in a particular decision. What happens is that we get a better informed and better structured debate around the real risks following from a particular decision. I do not wish to claim that we have reached perfection in this field; it is a continuous process of development.

Professor Fells

It seems to me that too enthusiastic a view of multi-scenario planning can be dangerous. I will choose an example where it was used by the British Government. The Department of Energy provided evidence at the Sizewell Enquiry in which it tried to look ahead to see what kind of demand for energy we were likely to encounter in the future. It put forward eight possible scenarios, covering such a wide range that it seemed to me that the document was useless. So there is the danger that if you choose too many scenarios, there is a problem over what you do with the information at the end of the day.

Mr Galer

To be of practical use this whole approach has to be kept simple. Without wishing to comment on the Department of Energy's scenarios, I should make it clear that we would try not to have more than three — and preferably not more than two — scenarios. So there is a balance there between intellectual rigour, where we no doubt lose out through a simplified approach, and practical value — which requires that the whole approach has to be kept simple.

Chairman

In a sense big companies must be able by their own actions to generate scenarios — or at least to vary a particular scenario. Does this aspect come into your thinking?

Mr Galer

I think that most of us, at least in my company, would believe that that is not really true. Although we may be big, we are not big enough to make significant changes. What can, and does, happen is that through the kind of analysis I have been describing, we may see certain trends developing that are either attractive or unattractive to us. We might then seek to influence other people's views, making representations to the Government or to other actors in the oil industry who may be in a position to change the situation. I must stress, however, that we do not affect the scenario ourselves.

Question

I would like to ask a question about a rather different uncertainty which has not figured very much in calculations for planning and forecasting. It relates to the Soviet Bloc. Am I right in thinking that the graphs of production and consumption in the Soviet Bloc countries are now crossing, and that they are moving into deficit at their present rate of production capacity? What effect does this, if it is true, have on the interests of the Gulf producers or, indeed, of other producers?

Dr Al-Chalabi

It is difficult to make judgements about the oil industry in the Soviet Union because information is extremely limited. There are some indications which would suggest that the expansion in the oil industry in the Soviet Union has come to a sort of halt and that it is not easy for the Soviet oil industry to expand any further. The difficulties that have been faced by the Soviet Union in keeping up production in certain important oil fields, for example, appear to be the result of real technical limitations to the oil fields; this suggests that the oil industry cannot go on expanding in the same way as it did over the last ten years. On the other hand, the oil exports from the Soviet Union are crucial to the country's achievement of a favourable balance of payments. As the Soviet Union is so dependent on the foreign exchange accruing from oil sales, it is not very likely that the Soviet Union will soon withdraw as an important exporter of oil. As a centrally planned economy, with a variety of energy resources, the Soviet government will probably ensure that the limitation which is now more and more indicated in the oil industry is not translated into a drastic reduction of oil exports. It could be met by reducing consumption of oil in favour of other sources of energy — they have, for example, enormous reserves of gas.

For some time to come, therefore, I believe that the Soviet oil industry will not be expanding, but that this will not be at the expense of their exports. They will continue to be significant exporters of oil and any shortfall in local production, in the domestic production of oil, will be met by an increase in the consumption of other sources of energy — gas, coal and even nuclear-generated electricity.

IV NATIONAL ACCOUNTING AND INCOME ILLUSION OF PETROLEUM EXPORTS: THE CASE OF THE ARAB GULF CO-OPERATION COUNCIL MEMBERS (AGCC)*

by Dr A.T. Al-Sadik**
Director of Research, Arab Monetary Fund, Abu Dhabi

Introduction

The traditional framework of national accounts does not distinguish between the contributions of depleting resources and those of reproducible ones to national income. This could be attributed to the fact that the fundamental framework for national accounts is the outcome of the intellectual work of Western economists and statisticians, who were influenced by the needs of the economies of the developed countries in which depleting resources did not significantly contribute to their economic activity. Besides, the economists and statisticians, who were involved in laying the groundwork for the national accounts, were interested in having a framework which would facilitate testing and applying Keynes's macroeconomic analysis. Such analysis was built around the two variables: national income and expenditures.

As the traditional framework of national accounts does not take into consideration the special character of the economies of oil exporting countries, its application to these countries is inappropriate. The application of the national accounts framework to countries whose economic mainstay depends on a depleting resource leads to confusing the two concepts of wealth and income. Such confusion leads to income illusion about proceeds of petroleum exports.

The income illusion shows up in:

Overestimation in national income level.

* Arab Gulf Co-operation Council (AGCC) members are: Bahrain, Kuwait, Oman, Qatar, Saudi Arabia and the United Arab Emirates.
** The views expressed here are those of the writer, and not necessarily those of the Arab Monetary Fund.

Overestimation in national savings.
Distortion in the current account position.
Underestimation in the domestic absorption.
Overestimation in the accumulation of national wealth.
Underestimation of foreign aid.
Distortion of the contributions of the different sectors to the national income.

In Section 1, I discuss the information content of some macro aspects of the traditional national accounts framework and the role of petroleum exports within the framework. In Section 2, the concepts of wealth and income are discussed and some aspects of the wealth-income relationship are presented. In Section 3, I discuss income from petroleum based on the given wisdom that petroleum is a depleting asset and a central concept of income. In Section 4, I present estimates of income from proceeds of petroleum exports; and in Section 5, a discussion of the consequences of the income illusion of proceeds of petroleum exports is taken up. A conclusion and two appendices are included. Appendix 1 presents an example of calculating net income from an oil well on the basis of the 1913 American Taxation Law, and Appendix 2 presents ratios of income to proceeds of petroleum for five AGCC members.

1. National Income and Petroleum: The Traditional National Accounts Framework

Macro Aspects of the Traditional National Accounts Framework

Given the magnitudes of consumption, investment, exports and imports of a country, then it is a simple matter of applying arithmetical operations to determine income in the context of the Traditional National Accounts Framework (TNAF). This is explicitly brought out by the income determination identity:

Income = Consumption + Investment
+ Exports − Imports

Income is either consumed or saved. That is,

Income = Consumption + Saving

Thus, a saving determination identity is deduced:

Saving = Income − Consumption

Consumption and investment variables refer to both private and public (government) sectors.

The preceding two forms of income identities lead to the following identity:

Saving − Investment = Exports − Imports

Domestic absorption is defined as the sum of Consumption and Investment. That is:

Domestic Absorption = Consumption + Investment

For brevity in the sequel, the following symbols are defined:

Symbol	Variable
Y	Income
C	Consumption
S	Saving
I	Investment
X	Total Exports
XO	Petroleum Exports
XN	Total Exports Less Petroleum Exports
M	Total Imports
A	Domestic Absorption (Domestic Expenditure)

Utilising the above symbols, the preceding identities take the following forms:

Income Identity
$$Y = C + I + X - M \qquad (1)$$
Saving Identity
$$S = Y - C \qquad (2)$$
Saving − Investment, Export − Import Identity
$$S - I = X - M \qquad (3)$$
Domestic Absorption Identity
$$A = C + I \qquad (4)$$
Identities (1) and (4) lead to another identity, namely:
$$Y - A = X - M \qquad (5)$$

Information Content of the Macro Identities in the Context of the TNAF. Interest here is in the information content of identities (3) and (5). Identity (3) states that the difference between saving and domestic investment (domestic resources balance) is identical to the difference between exports and imports (current account, goods and services). Similarly, identity (5) shows that the difference between income and domestic absorption (domestic balance) is identical to the current account.

The domestic balance $(Y - A)$ during a specified period can take one and only one of three states, namely:

(a) Y is greater than A; this implies that there is a surplus in the domestic balance

(b) Y is less than A; this implies that there is a deficit in the domestic balance

(c) Y is equal to A; this implies that there is an equilibrium in the domestic balance.

Corresponding to every state of the domestic balance, there is one state for the current account and one state for the domestic resource balance. Thus, a surplus in the domestic balance (Y greater than A) corresponds to a surplus in the current account (X greater than M) and a surplus in the domestic resource balance (S greater than I).

The information content in a surplus in the domestic balance is that domestic absorption (Consumption and Investment) is incapable of utilising the final goods and services generated in the economy implied by income during the specified period. Hence, the external sector, through trade, plays the role of a vent for surplus, following Adam Smith terminology, leading into a current account surplus. Moreover, a surplus in the domestic balance shows up in a surplus in the domestic resource balance; that is, saving exceeds the needs of domestic investment. Consequently, such surplus is reflected in an outflow in the form of direct and indirect investments.

Similarly, a deficit in the domestic balance (Y less than A) corresponds to a deficit in both the current account (X less than M), and the domestic resource balance (S less than I). The information content in such a state is that the final goods and services generated by the economy during the specified period run short of satisfying the needs of domestic absorption. Hence, the external sector emerges as a source for importing goods and services to fill the gap in the domestic balance. This leads into a deficit in the current account. Besides, a deficit in the domestic balance is reflected in a deficit in the domestic resource balance (saving runs short of domestic investment needs). Consequently, the external sector becomes a source for an inflow of resources to cover such a gap.

Avenues for the Disposition (Financing) of a Current Accounts Surplus (Deficit). A current account surplus in a country's balance of payments requires disposition. Choices for a country to handle the surplus could be the following:[1]

    (i) increase its international reserves;
   (ii) invest in foreign countries, both direct and indirect;
  (iii) lend to other countries and international and regional institutions;
  (iv) offer aid to other countries and foreign institutions.

However, choices for a country to finance its current account deficit could be the following:

    (i) use of its international reserves, if available;
   (ii) borrowing from international financial markets and/or international and regional institutions;
  (iii) obtaining aid from other countries and institutions;
  (iv) attraction of inflow of capital (private and public) for domestic investment;
   (v) exchange part of the national wealth for foreign financial assets.

An observation at this point is in order. All the choices listed above, whether in the case of surplus or deficit, may not be available for the country. Availability of a choice and utilising it are determined by both domestic and international factors. Such factors include a country's view of the interaction of its political and economic relations with the international community; and the impact of any available choice on its political and economic situation.

Choice (v) in the case of a deficit might seem far fetched. However, many petroleum exporting countries have been doing that, without explicitly admitting it due to the confinements of the TNAF. In this regard, Keynes's observation[2]

    ... the ideas of economists and political philosophers, both when they are right and when they are wrong, are more powerful than is commonly understood. Indeed the world is ruled by little else. Practical men, who believe themselves to be quite exempt from any intellectual influences, are usually the slaves of some defunct economist.

is revealing if one were to question the application of the TNAF to petroleum exporting countries.

Petroleum Exports in the Context of the TNAF

The practised application of the TNAF considers proceeds of petroleum exports as a part of the income of petroleum producing and exporting countries. This is illustrated as follows:

$$X = XO + XN \dots\dots\dots\dots\dots (6)$$

where XO stands for petroleum exports and XN for other exports. Substituting for X in (1) we get:

$$Y = C + I + XO + XN - M$$
or $$\qquad\qquad\qquad\dots\dots (7)$$
$$Y = A + XO + XN - M$$

Identity (7) shows that petroleum exports are considered a component of income Y.

Excluding petroleum exports from identity (7) results in:

$$Y - XO = A + XN - M \dots\dots\dots\dots (8)$$

The left hand side of (8) is income reduced by petroleum exports, which will be referred to as *truncated income* and donated by YN. Thus, (8) may take the form:

$$YN - A = XN - M \dots\dots\dots\dots (9)$$

Taking into consideration the new variable, YN, identity (2) may be put as follows:

$$S = Y_N + XO - C \dots\dots\dots\dots (10)$$

Identities (9) and (5): An Export Look at the Arab Gulf Co-operation Council Members. Comparison between the truncated income (YN) and the domestic absorption (A) for individual AGCC members shows that YN was less than (A) during several years (Table 4.1).

Table 4.1: Gross Domestic Product, Domestic Absorption, Petroleum Exports, Truncated Gross Domestic Product and Consumption for Members of Arab Gulf Co-operation Council ($US Millions)

	1975	1979	1980	1981	1982
Kuwait					
Y	12,017	23,324	27,209	25,211	21,226
A	5,469	11,135	15,828	16,022	17,910
XO	7,886	16,779	18,234	14,915	7,585
YN	4,131	6,545	9,875	10,296	13,641
C	3,938	9,601	10,656	12,015	13,330
Oman					
Y	2,097	3,395	5,562	6,770	6,350
A	1,743	2,635	4,014	5,071	5,937
XO	1,439	2,152	3,281	4,403	4,099
YN	658	1,243	2,281	2,367	2,251
C	996	1,714	2,670	3,442	4,115
Qatar					
Y	2,290	3,944	5,925	6,202	8,385
A	891	1,608	1,647	1,982	5,808
XO	1,757	3,577	5,387	5,316	3,988
YN	533	367	538	886	4,397
C	441	816	870	904	4,781
Saudi Arabia					
Y	39,688	73,932	107,249	137,045	146,189
A	14,896	60,413	69,838	91,807	108,662
XO	27,690	58,750	102,110	113,330	75,853
YN	11,889	15,182	5,139	23,715	70,336
C	9,651	39,499	47,612	55,924	60,042
United Arab Emirates					
Y	9,961	21,045	29,557	31,157	29,657
A	5,436	13,812	16,611	17,983	20,908
XO	6,726	12,862	19,454	18,740	15,463
YN	3,235	8,183	10,103	12,417	14,194
C	2,392	6,511	8,351	9,688	11,806

Note: Y = Gross Domestic Product.
        A = Domestic Absorption.
        XO = Petroleum Exports.
        YN = Y − XO.
        C = Consumption.

Source: AMF, *National Accounts of Arab Countries: 1971-1982*, IMF, *IFS*, various issues.

Therefore domestic absorption was high in relation to the truncated income, and hence a deficit in the current account was realised in relation to non-petroleum exports. Comparison between consumption (C) and the truncated income (YN) shows that (C) was greater than (YN) over a number of years (Table 4.1).

However, comparison between income (Y) and domestic absorption (A), and income (Y) and consumption (C) for each member of the AGCC reverses the results obtained when (YN) is involved (Table 4.1).

The message of the simple comparison exercise that has been presented is this: domestic absorption is low or high, realising a surplus or deficit in the current accounts, and accumulation or erosion of capital of the members of the AGCC are subject to the constraints of the TNAF, which treats petroleum exports as part of a country's national income. The issue implied in this connection explicitly is the following: Does economic theory support the practice of considering petroleum exports as part of national income? Before discussing the question, it is appropriate at this point to mention that petroleum is a depleting resource (asset); and research on some economic aspects of depleting resources is available in the literature. Studies consider petroleum an *asset* and component of *national wealth*.[3] However, available literature does not provide for an agreed upon procedure to make adjustments in the application of the TNAF to the economies of petroleum exporting countries.

Given that petroleum is an asset, then considering the proceeds of petroleum exports as a part of national income leads into a conceptual confusion between national wealth and income generated from wealth on the one hand, and between asset and income on the other. Such a conceptual confusion is not an 'intellectual entertainment', but is a serious issue embodied with implications and signals for making policies and taking decisions that affect several important variables that have national, regional and international significance.

Thus, an attempt to adjust the TNAF to take into consideration the distinction between national wealth and national income requires a discussion of the relationship between wealth and income. This is attempted in the following section.

2 Wealth and Income

Wealth Concept

Economic literature distinguishes between the two kinds of macro-economic variables, namely stocks and flows on the basis of time dimensions. Stocks are time-less concepts. A stock must be specified at a particular moment. Flows, however, have time dimensions; so much per period.[4]

Wealth is a stock concept. For example, we say, Mr Ram's wealth was W million dirhams at 30/6/1982, and wealth of country 'Sonny' amounted to W billion dinars at 30/6/1982. The stock of wealth of a country comprises property rights of material holdings (material capital) and human capital. In this chapter, wealth refers only to material wealth.

Wealth consists of:[5]

(a) Reproducible structures, and durable and consumable commodities.
(b) Non-reproducible, such as land, and hydro carbon resource.
(c) Financial foreign assets.

Non-reproducible are of two types: depleting assets (oil, gas) and non-depleting (land).

National wealth could be classified into two components, namely:

(1) Domestic assets, both reproducibles and non-reproducibles that are physically located within the boundaries of the country.
(2) Foreign assets, consisting of material assets (direct investments) in foreign countries and foreign financial assets.

Thus, it is convenient to present the components of national wealth as follows:

National Wealth = Domestic Assets + Foreign Assets
= Domestic Reproducible Assets
+ Domestic Non-reproducible Assets
+ Material Foreign Assets
+ Financial Foreign Assets

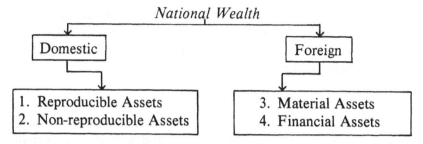

The preceding presentation on the wealth concept and the components of national wealth brings out the *income illusion* of proceeds of petroleum exports.

Petroleum is a domestic non-reproducible asset; its extraction decreases this wealth component. Exporting petroleum increases the wealth component of foreign financial assets. Thus the process of extracting petroleum reshuffles the components of national wealth in the first instance. The pattern of allocation of the increase in foreign financial assets determines the changes in national wealth and the national income generated thereof.

Income

Income is a flow concept. We say, for example, that 'Ram's' income in 1982 amounted to Z dirhams; and income of country 'Sonny' was L million dinars.

In the context of the TNAF, income of a country is the value of final economic goods and services it produces during a specified period. The process of production of the relevant goods and services entails participation and co-operation of the following factors of production:

(1) Land
(2) Labour
(3) Capital
(4) Entrepreneurship (Organisation).

Besides, technology plays a role in production and implicitly participates through the chosen technique of production implied by the production function.

Factors of production are compensated for their participation in the process: rent is allocated for land: labour receives wages, capital gets return (interest): and entrepreneurship gets profit. Production factors offer their services in the production process. Since such factors are components of wealth (capital and land being material wealth, and labour and organisation being human capital (wealth)), it follows that the relationship of wealth to production (consequently income) is that income is generated by services of wealth.

Relationship of Income to Wealth

Services rendered by factors of production, themselves components of wealth, are the link between income and wealth. For example, services of agricultural land, labour and capital (machines) produce crops, which in turn partially determine income from the land; also capital services combined with labour services produce vehicles, which in turn determine income from the factory. If we were to follow the preceding logic and apply it to determine income from petroleum, we would find out that what applies to the land or to the factory, does not apply to petroleum as it is a depleting asset. Therefore, calculating income from a depleting resource requires different logic. We may refer in this respect to the relevant parts of the 1913 American Taxation Law which indicates a procedure for calculating income from a depleting asset.

Income from a depleting asset is a function of the following variables:

(1) Sale price
(2) Sale volume
(3) Sale and extraction cost
(4) Decrease in the value of the depleting asset.

The first three variables have no special significance for a depleting asset; however, the fourth variable is of special importance. Thus the 1913 American Taxation Law includes a procedure to calculate depletion deduction for income tax purposes. The procedure is as follows:

1. The value of the property upon acquisition is taken as a basis and divided by the number of units of material estimated to have been in the ground at that time. That is,

unit of depletion = value of acquisition
÷ volume of reserves

2. Annual depletion deduction is calculated by multiplying the number of units extracted in a year by 'unit of depletion'.

3. The total of depletion deductions over the life of asset is the sum of

the annual deductions, provided that this sum does not exceed the original value of the property.

Taking into consideration the procedure above, income from a depleting asset is estimated from the following formula:

> Net income = value of sales − cost of production
> and   sales − depletion deduction

An example for calculating income from an oil well is provided in Appendix 1. The example shows that income from an oil well is a 'residual income'; it is what remains after deduction for depletion and costs of production and sales are made. Thus, such income could be negative as in the first and sixth years.

The procedure implied in the 1913 American Tax Law is simple and straightforward. However, its application to calculate income from the petroleum resource faces the problem of specifying an appropriate value of the resource. Relevant literature indicates that the value of an asset could be considered equivalent to the present value of a stream of receipts generated by the asset. Thus, if an asset gives rise to a stream of revenues (receipts):

$$R_1, R_2, \ldots \ldots R_i, R_n$$

where R_i represents revenue in year i, and n represents the number of years the asset generates revenues. Assuming that interest rates expected to prevail during the relevant years are:

$$r_1, r_2, \ldots \ldots r_i, r_n;$$

then the present value of the stream of receipts is:

Present value = $R_1 + [R_2/(1+r_1)(1+r_2)] + \ldots \ldots$

(P) $+ [R_i/(1+r_1)(1+r_2) \ldots (1+r_i)]$

$+ \ldots + [R_n/(1+r_1)(1+r_2)(1+r_n)]$

If the interest rate is constant over time at some level r, then the formula for present value takes the form:

$$P = R_1 + [R_2/(1+r)^2] + [R_i/(1+r)^i] + [R_n/(1+r)^n]$$

If receipts are constant at level R, then,

$$P = R \, [1-(1/1+r)^n] / 1 - (1/1+r) \; \ldots \ldots \; (11)$$

If receipts are constant at level R and continue indefinitely over time, then,

$$P = R / (1-1/1+r) \; \ldots \ldots \ldots \ldots \ldots \ldots \; (12)$$

The exercise above indicates that it is possible at a theoretical plane to estimate a value for the known petroleum reserves of a country. Utilising such a value and applying the outlined procedure in the 1913 American Tax Law lead to an estimate for income from petroleum exports. Such income is not equal to the proceeds of petroleum exports. Income from proceeds of petroleum exports is discussed in the next section.

3 Income from Petroleum

A basic concern of the AGCC members is to develop income generating activities to replace the flow of petroleum proceeds as the reserves are depleted. Thus if petroleum reserves are assumed to last (n) years, then the issue is how to transform a stream of receipts lasting (n) years into an infinite stream of receipts.

In order to discuss such issues, we refer again to the concept of income. An interesting and relevant discussion on the concept of income is in Hicks's *Value and Capital*.

> The purpose of income calculations in practical affairs is to give people an indication of the amount which they can consume without impoverishing themselves. Following out this idea, it would seem that we ought to define a man's income as the maximum value which he can consume during a week, and still expect to be as well off at the end of the week as he was at the beginning.[8]

Though Hicks discusses three aspects of income that are approximations to the central meaning of income quoted above, it is sufficient for our purpose to deal with one definition based on the central meaning of income. Thus, based on the concept of an individual's income, we define income from proceeds of petroleum exports (proceeds) as: the maximum value the country can consume without impoverishing itself in the future. To estimate the maximum value, given the proceeds, let C_1 stand for the maximum value the country can consume from the proceeds R without impoverishing itself. That is, income from petroleum exports is assumed to be C_1. The objective of the country is to continue to receive the value C_1 long after petroleum is depleted. The present value of an infinite stream at level C_1 is:

$$P_1 = C_1/1 - 1/1+r$$

That is,

$$P_1 = C_1(1+r/r) \dots \dots \dots \dots \dots \dots (13)$$

where r stands for a constant interest rate.

   If it is assumed that proceeds continue at level R for n years, then the present value of the stream of proceeds for n years is:

$$P_2 = R\,(1+r/r)\,[1-(1/1+r)^n] \dots \dots \dots (14)$$

To estimate C_1 in terms of R the finite stream represented in (14) is equated to the infinite stream represented in (13). Thus:

$$C_1 = [1-(1/1+r)^n]R \dots \dots \dots \dots (15)$$

Given the time span of the petroleum reserves (n) and the interest rate (r) and the annual proceeds (R), income (C_1) from the proceeds is estimated in formula (15).

   It is appropriate at this point to make a few remarks:

(1) Income (C_1) from proceeds is less than the proceeds.
(2) The ratio C_1/R is a function of the life span (n) of the reserves and the interest rate r.
(3) The ratio C_1/R is directly related to n; that is, the greater n is, the higher is the ratio C_1/R.
(4) Similarly the ratio C_1/R is directly related to r.
(5) So far nothing has been mentioned with respect to the nature of the values of the variables. However, based on the central concept of income, values should be in real terms. Having said

this, it is appropriate to point out that the main features and conclusions of the analysis are invariant with respect to the nature of variables (real or nominal).

In the next section, application of formula (15) is utilised to calculate income C_1 for the AGCC members.

4 Income from Petroleum Exports in the AGCC Members

Depletion of Oil Reserves

Time span for depletion of oil reserves (n) is a function of two variables, namely:

(a) Volume of proved oil reserves (OR),
(b) Annual oil production (OP).

Given OR and OP, then the number of years oil reserves will last is given by:

$$n = OR/OP \dots\dots\dots (16)$$

AGCC members' proved crude oil reserves at the end of 1981 were estimated at 273.8 billion barrels; and their combined crude oil production amounted to 4,793.6 million barrels in 1981.[9] Assuming 1981 production level as an average for future production, then the crude oil reserves of the AGCC members would be depleted in 57 years. Table 4.2 presents reserves, production and time span for oil depletion in five AGCC members.

The time span for oil depletion variable (n) is elastic with respect to production and reserves; a 1 per cent increase in production (reserves) decreases (increases) the time span by 1 per cent.

Estimation of Income from Oil in the AGCC Members

Formula (15) shows that the ratio of C_1 to R, i.e. C_1:R depends on two variables; n, the number of years oil reserves last and r, the interest rate (the discount factor). n is given in Table 4.2. Thus the variable r determines the level of the ratio C_1:R.

I assume that r ranges between 0.5 per cent and 10 per cent for the purpose of the exercise. Calculations of C_1:R is carried out for

$$r = 0.5 + i, \ i = 0, 0.5, 1, 1.5, \dots\dots, 9.5.$$

Table 4.2: Crude Oil Reserves, Oil Production and Time Span for Oil Depletion in AGCC Members

	Reserves at 31/12/1981 (billion barrels) (1)	Production in 1981 (million barrels) (2)	Oil Depletion (Years) (3) = (1) ÷ (2)
Kuwait	67.75[a]	408.1[a]	166
Oman	2.6	116.1	22
Qatar	3.4	147.8	23
Saudi Arabia	167.85[a]	3,580.7[a]	47
United Arab Emirates	32.2	540.8	60
Total	273.8	4,793.6	57

Note: a. Including share from neutral zone.
Source: *Oil and Energy Trends, Statistical Review, 1983*, Tables 1-1 and 3-1.

That is, r takes a minimum of 0.5 per cent, increasing by 0.5 per cent up to a maximum of 10 per cent.

The results of the exercise are displayed in Appendix 2. The results are consistent with what has been pointed out concerning the sensitivity of the ratio C_1:R to n and r.

Given n = 166 years for Kuwait, the ratio C_1:R is estimated to be 56 per cent for r = 0.5 per cent; 81 per cent, 96 per cent and 99 per cent for r equal to 1 per cent, 2 per cent and 3 per cent respectively. For Saudi Arabia, the ratio C_1:R is lower for the corresponding values of r due to the fact that time span for depletion of reserves in Saudi Arabia is shorter (47 years). A glance at Figure 4.1 of the ratios C_1:R for the five members of the AGCC shows that the lowest ratio is that for Qatar and highest one for Kuwait. Given the interest rate the level of the ratio is a function of n.

In the absence of detailed and accurate data for rates of return on investments of proceeds of petroleum exports, any assumption about interest rates is subject to questioning. However, interest rates on deposits in commercial banks and on treasury bills in Western industrial countries could be taken as indicators for nominal rates of return on the investment. Comparison of the nominal rates with inflation rates in the relevant countries indicates an appropriate level for real interest rates.

At this point, it might be indicative to mention that a study on *The Role and Management of Current Account Surpluses of the Oil Producing Countries of the Arabian Peninsula* finds that the long-

Figure 4.1: Ratios of Income to Proceeds of Petroleum Exports (k)

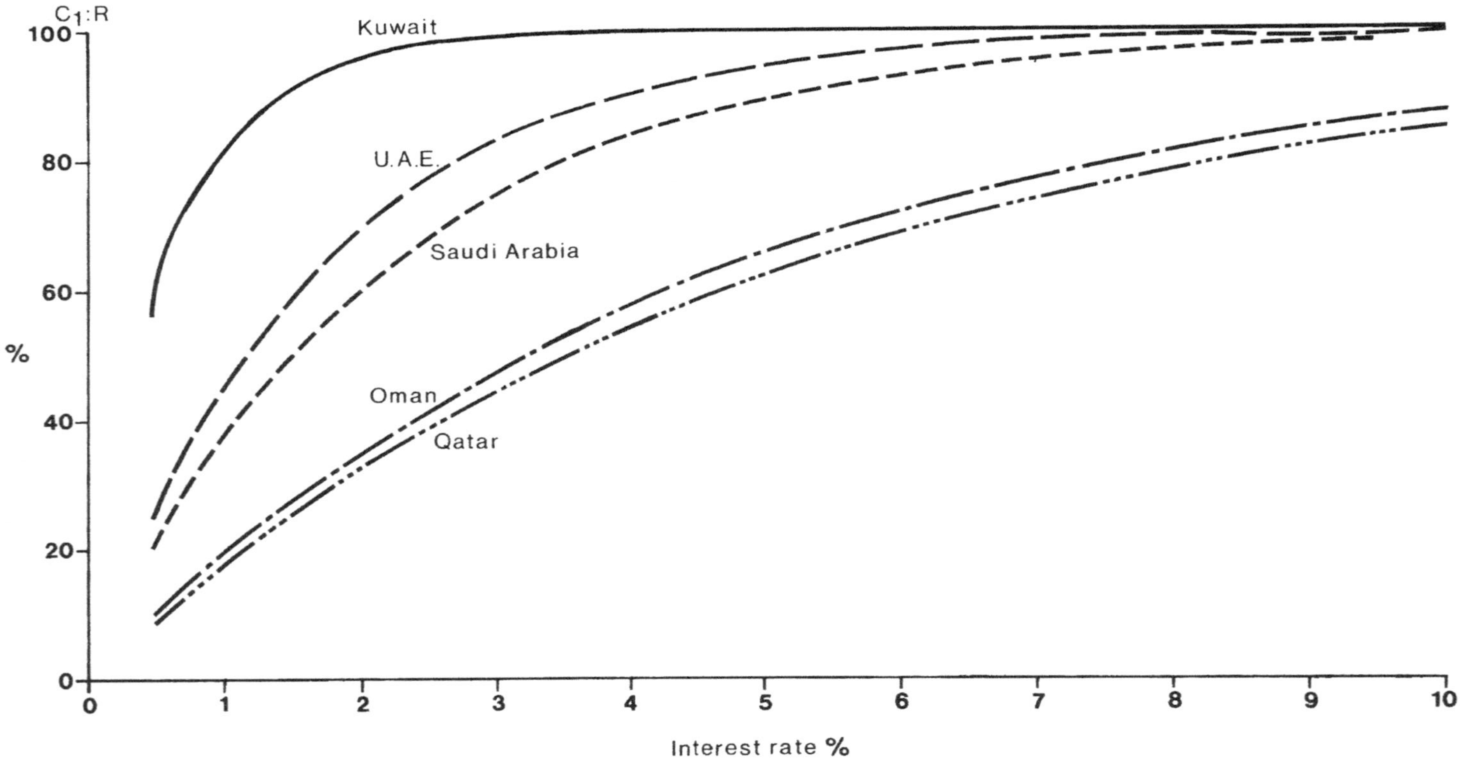

term US government bonds return 3.0 per cent per year compounded annually over the period (1926-81). However, the inflation adjusted annual return for the same was negative 0.1 per cent. For similar maturity of corporate bonds and over the same period, inflation-adjusted annual return was 0.5 per cent. For US Treasury bills over the same period, the annual real return was zero.[10]

Based on the preceding indicators, I choose two reference real interest rates, a minimum of 0.5 per cent and a maximum of 1.5 per cent, to estimate two corresponding ratios of income (C_1) to petroleum proceeds R. The estimates for five AGCC members are presented in Table 4.3.

Table 4.3: Ratios: Income (C_1) to Proceeds of Petroleum Exports (R): $C_1 : R$

	Time Span for Depletion of Reserves as of 31/12/1981 (years)	Real Interest Rate	
		0.5 per cent $C_1 : R$	1.5 per cent $C_1 : R$
Kuwait	166	56.30	91.55
Qatar	23	10.83	28.99
Saudi Arabia	47	20.89	50.32
United Arab Emirates	60	25.86	59.07
Oman	22	10.39	27.93

Source: Time Span for Depletion of Reserves from Table 4.2. Ratios from Appendix 2.

To complete the exercise, I consider estimates of proceeds of petroleum exports and apply the two ratios presented in Table 4.3 for each of the five AGCC members. Column (1) in Table 4.4 presents the petroleum proceeds in 1982. Column (2) lists the ratio $(C_1 : R)$ for r = 0.5 per cent and Column (3) gives income C_1. Columns (4) and (5) repeat the same for r = 1.5 per cent. I use the estimates for income (C_1) from petroleum proceeds to adjust the estimates for conventional income (GDP). To do this, it is helpful to repeat here that there are three estimates for some kinds of income, namely the conventional one Y; the truncated income YN, which is Y minus petroleum proceeds; and C_1, the maximum amount that can be consumed from petroleum proceeds without impoverishing the country.

I introduce here the adjusted income Y*. Y* is equal to YN plus C_1; that is

$$Y^* = YN + C_1$$

or $\qquad\qquad\qquad\qquad\qquad\qquad\qquad\qquad$ (17)

$$Y^* = (Y - XO) + C_1$$

Table 4.4: Income C_1 from the Proceeds of Petroleum Exports in 1982 ($US Millions)

	Petroleum Proceeds	Ratio C_1:R (r=0.5)	Income C_1	Ratio C_1:R (r=1.5)	Income C_1
	(1)	(2)	(3)=(1)x(2)	(4)	(5)=(1)x(4)
Kuwait	7,585	56.30	4,270	91.55	6,944
Oman	4,099	10.39	426	27.93	1,145
Qatar	3,988	9.49	378	25.75	1,027
Saudi Arabia	75,853	20.89	15,846	50.32	38,169
United Arab Emirates	15,463	25.86	3,999	59.07	9,134

Source: Proceeds from IMF, *IFS*, January 1984.

Table 4.5 presents estimates for Y, XO, YN, C_1 and the adjusted income Y^* for r = 0.5 per cent and r = 1.5 per cent in 1982.

Comparison between the conventional income (Y) and the adjusted income (Y^*) shows the overestimation in income levels for the members of the AGCC in the context of the TNAF. Thus considering all petroleum export proceeds as income is inconsistent with the accepted wisdom that petroleum is an asset. This inconsistency within the TNAF leads to 'illusion' about the income of the country concerned, which has consequences on the country's view of its economy and its international relations. This issue is taken up in the next section.

5 Consequences of the Income Illusion of Petroleum Exports

Confusing the two concepts of wealth and income is the root of income illusion of petroleum exports. Several economic variables are affected by the income illusion of the proceeds of petroleum exports. The income illusion is reflected in overestimation of national income, national savings and national wealth; and it is also reflected in underestimation of domestic absorption and foreign aid; and in

Table 4.5: Adjusted Income (Y*) for the Members of AGCC in 1982 ($US Millions)

	Y (1)	YN (2)	C_1 (r = 0.5)	C_1 (r = 1.5)	Y* (r = 0.5)	Y* (r = 1.5)
Kuwait	21,226	13,641	4,270	6,944	17,911	20,585
Oman	6,350	2,251	426	1,145	2,677	3,396
Qatar	8,385	4,397	378	1,027	4,775	5,424
Saudi Arabia	146,189	70,336	15,846	38,169	86,182	108,505
United Arab Emirates	29,657	14,194	3,999	9,134	18,193	23,328

Sources: AMF, *National Accounts for Arab Countries: 1971-1982*; Table 4.4.

distortion in the position of the current account and the sectoral structure of the national income. In the following I attempt to discuss the impact of the income illusion on each of these variables.

Exaggeration of National Income of Petroleum Exporting Countries

The exaggeration in national income of petroleum exporting countries is explicitly clear in identity (7):

$$Y = A + XO + XN - M \quad \ldots\ldots\ldots\ldots\ldots \quad (7)$$

Where proceeds of petroleum exports (XO) are considered as income, I have argued that only a portion of (XO) could be considered income. Thus, the truncated income YN underestimates national income. The other income defined in the paper is the adjusted income Y*. The levels of the three incomes Y, YN and Y* are ordered as:

$$YN < Y* \leqslant Y$$

Overestimating national income as reflected in Y, translates into higher levels of consumption. This is borne out by a simple version of consumption theory, which makes the level of consumption (C) as a function of the level of income Y, as in the following linear function:

$$C = a + bY \quad \ldots\ldots\ldots\ldots\ldots\ldots\ldots\ldots\ldots \quad (18)$$

where (b) represents the marginal propensity to consume. Because the TNAF overestimates the national income of the petroleum exporting countries in general, and the AGCC in particular (see Table 4.5), these countries allocate a higher portion of their inflated national incomes to consumption than would be the case if proceeds of petroleum exports were not viewed as income. This is clearly illustrated by Figure 4.2 in the income–consumption space. Since national income of a petroleum exporting country is inflated by an amount equivalent to $(Y - Y*)$, it induces extra consumption amounting to $b(Y - Y*)$, which is equal to the difference between ex-post consumption C and an ex-ante consumption C* based on the adjusted income Y*. It is important for the development of the economic base in the petroleum exporting countries that consumption C does not absorb all of the adjusted income Y*. For if C is more than

Figure 4.2

Consumption

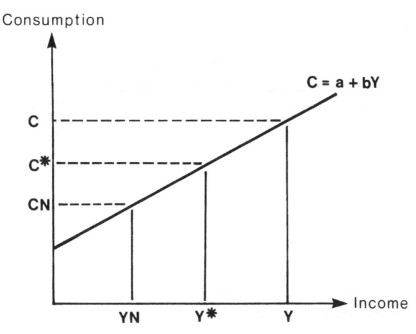

Y*, then the difference would be financed by the accumulated savings (national wealth). Such a situation would not be sustainable for very long. This could be illustrated by utilising a life-cycle income consumption paradigm. An individual passes through three stages during his lifetime. The first stage is characterised by dependence on others, and consumption is greater than income. Consumption is financed by the family or by borrowing. The second stage starts when the individual enters the labour market, and ends when he retires. This stage is characterised by the fact that income is more than consumption, so that savings take place. The third stage starts when the individual retires. The income-consumption relation in this stage is that consumption is greater than income and the excess is financed from savings. The three stages are illustrated in Figure 4.3.

When consumption C of an oil exporting country is greater than Y*, the adjusted income, then the country would be in stage I of a life-cycle model. However, an oil exporting country (or any country) would not be a viable economic and political entity in stage 1 in the long run. An economic and political entity would be viable and sustainable only if it positions itself in Stage II, where consumption is less than income. That is, there is saving to finance investments, which are basic to sustainable growth.

Figure 4.3

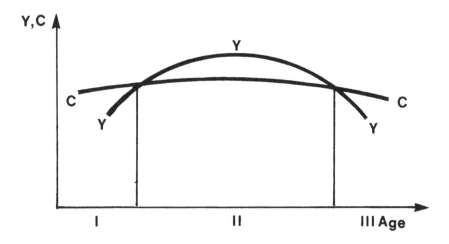

Overestimation of National Savings

National savings are equivalent to national income reduced by national consumption. That is,

$$S = Y - C$$

Assuming the linear relationship between consumption C and income Y as in (18), then:

$$S = -a + (1-b) \ Y \ \ldots\ldots\ldots\ldots\ldots\ldots\ldots \ (19)$$

Since the TNAF exaggerates Y for the petroleum exporting countries, it also exaggerates their national savings.

As national savings ex-post are necessarily equivalent to national investments (at home and abroad), national investments are also exaggerated. Thus since Y is greater than Y*, S is greater than S*, the savings that are realised when the adjusted income is considered. To see the consequence of the exaggeration in S, consider investments as a good to be produced by the services of labour and capital combined with the technology embodied in a production function. In the AGCC members, domestic investments are mostly produced by imported labour and physical capital. Savings finance the imported services of labour and capital.

Utilising the iso-cost and iso-quant aspects of Production Theory in microeconomics, savings S determine the levels of labour and capital employed in the investment process. To see this, let W represent the wage rate of labour and P prices of capital, then

$$wL + pK = S \quad \dots\dots\dots\dots\dots\dots\dots\dots \quad (20)$$

represents the iso-cost in the K — L plane where L represents the labour factor and K represents the capital factor. Figure 4.4 illustrates the point.

Figure 4.4

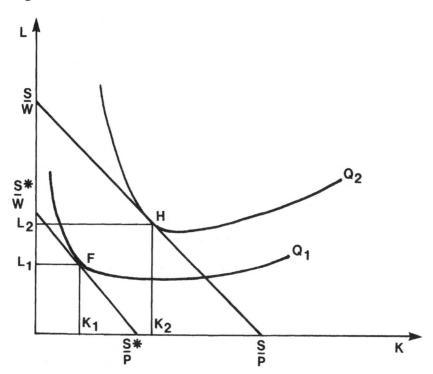

Since S is exaggerated, the investment good is produced at level Q_2 at H, requiring K_2 and L_2 units of capital and labour respectively. In comparison the S* savings corresponding to the adjusted income produce the investment good at level Q_1 at F, requiring K_1 and L_1 units of capital and labour respectively. Thus, exaggeration in the national savings induces higher levels of imports of labour and capital.

Underestimation of Domestic Absorption

The claim that domestic absorption of a country is low or high is void of informative content because 'low' or 'high' are relative terms. Domestic absorption is low or high relative to another variable. The implied variable in the literature is national income. Since the TNAF overestimates the national income of a petroleum exporting country, its domestic absorption (A) is relatively underestimated. This is illustrated by data presented in Table 4.1, where (A) is higher than (YN), the truncated income, and also is illustrated by data in Tables 4.5 and 4.1 where domestic absorption in 1982 for most AGCC members exceeded the adjusted income Y*.

Distortion of the Current Account Position

Overestimation of the national income of a petroleum exporting country leads to misinformation about the domestic balance $(Y - A)$ which is reflected in the current account position $(X - M)$. Data in Table 4.1 show that the truncated income YN is less than domestic absorption over the period considered, that is $YN - A$ is negative. This implies that the current account excluding petroleum exports is in 'deficit', that is, $XN - M$ is negative. But, including petroleum exports, the current account becomes in a surplus position. Taking the adjusted income Y* for 1982, the current accounts of AGCC members are in deficit (Tables 4.1 – 4.5). Thus, the proceeds of petroleum exports financed the 'deficits'. Since it is argued that petroleum proceeds are a part of national wealth, then the 'deficits' were financed by a portion of national wealth.

Underestimation of Relative Foreign Aid Granted by AGCC Members

The fact that the TNAF exaggerates the national income of a petroleum exporting country is reflected in an underestimation of the portion of income donated to developing countries. This is the case because the conventional income Y is higher than the truncated income YN and the adjusted income Y*. Thus, the calculated ratio of concessional assistance to income Y is underestimated by the factor Y:Y*. For example, 1981 net disbursements as per cent of income as measured by gross national income for members of AGCC are reported as follows:[11]

Kuwait	1.98
Qatar	2.64
Saudi Arabia	4.66
United Arab Emirates	2.88

To illustrate the point, the ratio of income Y to the adjusted income Y* in 1982 as presented in Table 4.5 is calculated for the four donors. The ratios (Y:Y*) are:

	(r = 1.5)	(r = 0.5)
Kuwait	1.0311	1.185
Qatar	1.5459	1.7560
Saudi Arabia	1.3473	1.696
United Arab Emirates	1.2713	1.630

Applying these ratios to the preceding percentages, one gets:

	(r = 1.5)	(r = 0.5)
Kuwait	2.042	2.346
Qatar	4.081	4.636
Saudi Arabia	6.278	7.903
United Arab Emirates	3.661	4.694

The preceding exercise illustrates the underestimation in reporting relative foreign aid as a percentage of income.

Distortion of Relative Contribution of Sectors to National Income

As Y is exaggerated because it contains a 'wealth' component, the relative positions of the economic sectors of the economy are distorted. Distortions in the sectoral structure of the economy lead to wrong information signals about the performance of the sectors. Wrong signals are liable to induce misguided policies and decisions.

6 Conclusion

Petroleum is an *asset* and is a component of the material national wealth. Thus, extraction of petroleum and its exchange for foreign financial assets do not create income, but rather *reshuffle* the mix of national wealth. Accepting the preceding logic implies that application of the traditional national accounts framework to the economies of petroleum exporting countries confuses the two concepts of *wealth* and *income*. Such confusion between an asset and an income generated by an asset leads into overestimation and underestimation of key variables that have an impact on and influence the economic behaviour of countries and individuals. For example, income of the petroleum exporting countries is overestimated, so are the savings variable, and the position of the current account. Domestic absorption is underestimated, and the relative sectoral contributions to income are distorted. Besides, relative aid is underestimated.

To remedy the confusion between the two concepts of wealth and income, a relationship between wealth and income is derived. This relationship is utilised to estimate income generated from the proceeds of petroleum exports for five members of the Arab Gulf Co-operation Council.

Notes

1. A.P. Thirlwall, *Inflation, Saving and Growth in the Developing Countries*, Macmillan, London, 1974, p. 179.

2. J.M. Keynes, *The General Theory of Employment, Interest, and Money*, Harcourt, Brace and World, Inc. New York, First Harbinger Edn. 1964, p. 383.

3. See, for example, H. Hotelling, 'The Economics of Exhaustible Resources', *Journal of Political Economy*, vol. 39, no. 2 (1931), pp. 137-75; T.R. Stauffer, 'Measuring Oil Addiction: Growth Versus Expansion in a Rentier Economy', *Middle East Economic Survey*, vol. 14, no. 47 (7 September 1981); S.E. Al-Sairafy, 'Absorptive Capacity and Demand for Revenues and Petroleum Supply', *Oil and Arab Co-operation*, vol. 7, no. 2, 1981, pp. 61-81 (Arabic); A.T. Sadik, 'Patterns of Foreign Trade of Arab Producing and Exporting Petroleum and their Relations with the Future of Arab Development' in *Oil and Development Issues in the Arab World and their Relation to Global Economic Developments*, Seminar Proceedings 1978/79, Arab Planning Institute in Kuwait, pp. 119-75.

4. R.G.D. Allen, *Macro-Economic Theory: A Mathematical Treatment*, Macmillan, London, 1968, p. 2.

5. J. Kendrick, *Economic Accounts and their Uses*, McGraw Hill, New York, Ch. 2; I. Fisher, *The Nature of Capital and Income*, Augustus, M. Kelley, New York, 1965, Ch. 1.

6. Hotelling, 'The Economics of Exhaustible Resources', p. 170.

7. J. Hirshleifer, *Investment, Interest and Capital*, Prentice-Hall, Inc., Englewood Cliffs, NJ, 1970, ch. 2.

8. J.R. Hicks, *Value and Capital*, 2nd edn, Oxford University Press, Oxford, 1978, p. 172.

9. Bahrain, a member of AGCC, is not included in the figures.

10. Askari, Jalal and Sheshunoff International, *The Role and Management of Current Account Surpluses of the Oil Producing Countries of the Arabian Peninsula*, a study prepared for the Development Forum for Oil Producing Countries in the Arabian Peninsula, 1983, pp. 192-3.

11. OECD, *Aid from OPEC Countries*, Paris, 1983, p. 21, Table 11.2.

APPENDIX 1

Example of Calculating Net Income from an Oil Well: An Application of the 1913 American Taxation Law

An oil well with recoverable reserves of 500 million barrels was acquired for $5 billion. The well was depleted in nine years. the schedule of production and sales, sale price and values of sales were as shown in Table A.

Table A: Volume of Sales, Sale Price and Value of Sales

Year	Volume of Sales (million barrels) (1)	Sale Price ($/barrel) (2)	Value of Sales (million dollars) (3)
1	30	10	300
2	40	15	600
3	50	20	1,000
4	60	20	1,200
5	70	15	1,050
6	80	10	800
7	70	15	1,050
8	60	15	900
9	40	15	600

Calculating the net annual income from an oil well requires data on the following variables:

(a) Value of annual sales: this is given in column (3), Table A.
(b) Cost of production and sales: assume that the cost of production and sales of one barrel is equal to one dollar.
(c) Annual depletion deduction: this variable could be estimated from the given data as follows:

$$\text{per barrel depletion deduction} = \frac{\text{Acquisition Value of Well}}{\text{Volume of Reserves}}$$

$$= \frac{5,000}{500} = 10 \text{ dollars}$$

Thus, annual depletion deduction is equal to ten times volume of sales. Accordingly, annual cost of production and sales and annual depletion deduction are calculated as in Table B.

Table B: Production and Sales Cost and Depletion Deduction

Year	Vol. of sales Million barrels (1)	Cost of Prod and sales $ per barrel (2)	Depletion Deduction $ per barrel (3)	Cost of Prod and Sales (Million $) 4=(1)x(2)	Depletion Deduction (Million $) 5=(1)x(3)
1	30	1	10	30	300
2	40	1	10	40	400
3	50	1	10	50	500
4	60	1	10	60	600
5	70	1	10	70	700
6	80	1	10	80	800
7	70	1	10	70	700
8	60	1	10	60	600
9	40	1	10	40	400

The data required for calculating net income from an oil well are shown in Table A column (3) and Table B columns (4) and (5). Net income for each of the nine years is shown in Table C.

Table C: Net Income from an Oil Well (Million dollars)

Year	Annual Sales (1)	Annual Cost (2)	Annual Depletion (3)	Annual Net Income 4 = (1) – (2) – (3)
1	300	30	300	– 30
2	600	40	400	160
3	1,000	50	500	450
4	1,200	60	600	540
5	1,050	70	700	280
6	800	80	800	– 80
7	1,050	70	700	280
8	900	60	600	240
9	600	40	400	160

It is obvious from the exercise that net income from a depleting resource is a *residual income*; that is, it is the remaining portion of the proceeds of sales after allocation for cost and depletion.

APPENDIX 2

Ratios of Income (C_1) to Proceeds of Petroleum Exports (R)

Interest %	N^a	0.5	1.0	1.5	2.0	2.5	3.0	3.5	4.0	4.5	5.0
Country											
Kuwait	166	0.5630	0.8083	0.9155	0.9626	0.9834	0.9926	0.9967	0.9985	0.9993	0.9997
Oman	22	0.1039	0.1966	0.2793	0.3532	0.4191	0.4781	0.5308	0.5780	0.6203	0.6582
Qatar	23	0.1083	0.2046	0.2899	0.3658	0.4333	0.4933	0.5467	0.5943	0.6366	0.6744
Saudi Arabia	47	0.2090	0.3735	0.5033	0.6057	0.6867	0.7507	0.8015	0.8417	0.8737	0.8991
United Arab Emirates	60	0.2586	0.4496	0.5907	0.6952	0.7727	0.8303	0.8731	0.9049	0.9287	0.9465

Interest %	N^a	5.5	6.0	6.5	7.0	7.5	8.0	8.5	9.0	9.5	10.0
Country											
Kuwait	166	0.9999	0.9999	1.0000	1.0000	1.0000	1.0000	1.0000	1.0000	1.0000	1.0000
Oman	22	0.6921	0.7225	0.7498	0.7743	0.7963	0.8161	0.8338	0.8498	0.8642	0.8772
Qatar	23	0.7008	0.7382	0.7651	0.7891	0.8105	0.8297	0.8469	0.8622	0.8760	0.8883
Saudi Arabia	47	0.9193	0.9353	0.9482	0.9584	0.9666	0.9731	0.9784	0.9826	0.9860	0.9887
United Arab Emirates	60	0.9597	0.9697	0.9771	0.9827	0.9870	0.9901	0.9925	0.9943	0.9957	0.9967

Note: a. N = number of years for depletion of oil.

DISCUSSION

Discussant: Dr J. Presley, Department of Economics, University of Loughborough, England

I would like to thank Dr Sadik for an excellent paper. Let me make one or two comments. I have a great deal of sympathy with what Dr Sadik contends. His central point, as I understand it, is that the existing concept of national income, the one that economists and politicians enjoy using, is not really appropriate for the oil exporting countries. I agree with that and I would like to explain why. It is important to appreciate, first of all, what we use the national product for. The national product of the UK is simply a measure of the flow of income. All we do basically is to add together income, profits, rents and interest. The flow of income also represents the flow of the value of goods and services that we are producing in any one year. The whole concept, therefore, is a flow concept rather than a stock concept. Politicians and economists use national product and national income as measures of growing prosperity or increasing well-being. They talk about league tables and comparative rates of economic growth, comparing the UK at the bottom of the league table with other countries who are growing at 15 or 20 per cent per annum. So there is an international comparison.

A further use of the national product/income concept is to estimate *per capita* income. If we divide national income by the population, then we have a measure of the standard of living; and if we divide the national income by the labour force, then we have a measure of productivity — GDP per member of the labour force as an indicator of productivity.

I think the point that Dr Sadik is making is that we have now become habituated, and it is a bad habit, of also using national product as an indicator of the ability to create a flow of income in the future. Primarily the national income for 1983/4 is simply a measure of the flow of income in 1983/4, but we have grown used to thinking (as economists and politicians) that if we can produce that level of income this year, then we should automatically be able to produce at least as much next year and the year after. The concept of national income/product, however, simply measures the flow of income now and not in the future; we have to make a clear distinction between flow and stocks. It is the stock of wealth which reflects the country's ability to create more income in the future. It is the stock of human capital, physical capital and raw material reserves (in the case of the petroleum exporters, the amount of oil left in the ground) which determines the amount of income that is going to be generated in the future. If we want the national income to perform this task we need to deflate its value, as Dr Sadik has set about doing in his paper.

Now, what about the usefulness of the existing concept of national income for the oil exporting countries? If Kuwait or Saudi Arabia sell more oil abroad, they create more income in the form of profits accruing to the Government, wages and salaries, but that does not automatically mean that the people of Kuwait and Saudi Arabia are better off. The national income/product concept, therefore, is not fulfilling the function of measuring the standard of living. So it is not a good measure of the standard of living. To make a realistic estimate of growth in the standard of living, we would need to know something about the uses to which oil income is being put. It may take time for the benefit of oil income to accrue to the people of Kuwait and Saudi Arabia in the form of more imports, more schools, more hospitals, improved power supplies, desalinated water and so on.

Furthermore, the fact that more oil has been produced and sold, and as a result the national income per employee appears to have increased, does not mean that labour is necessarily more productive in Kuwait or Saudi Arabia because of that increase. The oil sector in Saudi Arabia obviously creates the major portion of national income, yet it employs only 36,000 people out of a total work force of 2½ million people. Increasing production of oil from five to ten million barrels per day does not give us cause to believe that the 2½ million Saudis and non-Saudis working in Saudi Arabia have suddenly grown more skilful and productive. Using national product to reflect productivity, therefore, is also misleading. Again we must deflate the existing national income concept. The usefulness of national product for oil-exporting countries as an indicator of economic progress and standards of living and productivity is very limited. In that I agree with Dr Sadik. So we need an alternative measure, we need to deflate the national income so that it can perform the task that the national income is supposed to perform, measuring standards of living, productivity and so on. The existing concept of national income can do no more than simply measure the flow of income over a period; that was what it was designed for, it does nothing more useful than that.

The application of Dr Sadik's approach to the oil economies does not preclude its application to other economies as well. Exporters of any raw material could argue the same case: exporters of copper, uranium, iron ore, etc. are in a similar position to oil exporters. In fact we could even reach the point where exporters of any type of wealth could argue the same case for deflating the national income. For example, exporters of human capital could contend that human capital is part of the wealth of the economy. Now, if we are going to apply the same sort of approach to all forms of wealth that are exported then our national accounting concept would be thrown into a fair amount of chaos. If, on the other hand, it is applied only to oil exporters, then the procedure would appear to be inconsistent.

A useful compromise might be to educate politicians and economists into mentioning the fall in the stock of wealth that may have taken place in a given year whenever they talk about the growth in national product. By all means, we should say, mention that in Saudi Arabia the economy is growing at 10 per cent per annum, but also mention that oil reserves have diminished by 'x' amount. People who accept your first statement will be able to appreciate that you have lost some potential for the future growth of income because you have depleted your oil reserves.

Chairman

It seems to me that you have been unfair on one point which Dr Sadik was making. He was not, surely, saying that everything that is exported should be counted according to his revised procedure. He was only referring to things which are not renewable. People are renewable, therefore, so long as we are all reproducing faster than we are exporting, it would not be fair to apply Dr Sadik's proposal to the export of human capital.

Dr Presley

Let me illustrate my point by a personal example. I worked in Saudi Arabia for a year in 1979. My working life, hopefully, is about 40 years, so for one-fortieth of my working life the skills which I possess were not available to my own country.

Dr Sadik

The basic point is that I was talking about a depleting non-renewable resource. Human beings are renewable.

It would of course be helpful if we could have a wealth statement for each of the Arab oil-producing countries, but that would probably be very difficult to compile. Even if one could, however, this would not remove the inconsistency in the national accounting procedure. The future viability of the oil-producing countries depends on them knowing exactly what they have and what to expect; that is why they need a new procedure for estimating national product and income.

Professor Sadler

Others have touched upon this problem of oil being part of the national asset structure and not part of income, but this has mostly been done so as to convince us in the West of the rectitude of the price of oil. What you have done is to turn the matter around and direct it at the oil economies themselves.

As you know, I have for some years been working on the Kuwait economy. I have taken the view that Kuwait, as other oil producing countries, has three sets of assets — all of which are in one portfolio. There is oil, internal investment and external investment. National planning becomes an exercise in portfolio management: the liquidation of oil should be translated into other parts of the portfolio, and unless the other parts of the portfolio grow at a faster rate than the fall in the value of the oil reserves the portfolio loses in overall value. How would you react to this approach?

Dr Sadik

The theme of my paper was that we really need to know what is available to us in the form of income and what is available in the form of assets being eaten up or consumed. I can see a clear link between the approach which Professor Sadler is suggesting and the concern of my paper. The portfolio approach does indeed make the connection between depletion of oil reserves and the overall wealth of the economy.

Dr Wilson

The fact is that no country has an estimation of its national wealth. The practicalities of trying to arrive at any kind of estimate are insuperable. For that reason I would suggest that Dr Sadik's approach, adjusting national income by leaving out oil income, is really more promising than the portfolio approach — which requires an overall estimate of national wealth.

Dr Sadik

I definitely agree with you that it is very difficult to estimate national wealth. Many industrial countries do not have wealth estimates, or wealth accounts. It is much simpler to stick to income and then to adapt the figures so as to make them realistic. The variables for oil-producing countries must include the expected return and the life span of the oil reserves. These are the easiest and most practical variables to use.

Dr Bridge

The problem as I see it is that the accounting concept, which is strictly concerned with assessment of past performance, has come over the last 20 years to be used in a predictive manner. National income accounts, thus, have come to be used to forecast growth of income, growth of GDP, growth of exports, etc.

On the wealth side, the immediate parallel is probably with an individual who has to live in a house full of old master paintings. In the same way as the oil producer releases onto the world market so many millions of barrels of oil per day, so the individual releases an oil painting onto the market every year. That person is depleting his assets: we are very clear about that. We are also clear that he has income and that it is actual money which he can spend or save. Bearing this comparison in mind, I am not at all sure that economists suffer from illusions as Dr Sadik says they do. In the accounting world, people receive income and spend it on a wide range of goods and services. Where does the illusion come in?

Dr Sadik

There is an illusion because you have an asset, a wealth component, which at the same time you are treating as an income. The proceeds of oil exports form a portion of your wealth.

CONCLUDING PANEL DISCUSSION

Chairman

I would like to start by asking Dr Al-Chalabi, who has listened and contributed throughout the Symposium, if he would give us the thoughts which are topmost in his mind. He will be followed by Dr El-Rumaihi and Mr Belgrave.

Dr Al-Chalabi

I believe that the objective of this meeting should be to create some ideas as to how we can achieve a greater degree of stability in the 1980s, now that the effects of the growing instabilities of the 1970s have led to major changes in the world economic and energy situation. The 1970s witnessed tumultuous developments which created a situation characterised by instability. The oil market has become more unpredictable and world economic problems have been growing both in the developed, and more especially the developing, countries.

I would like now to make a few points about the requirements for stability in the 1980s. Everyone must agree that the world needs some degree of continuity in its energy supplies and some stability in its energy costs. The producing countries, for their part, require some stability in oil revenue, so as to enable them to achieve reasonable rates of growth, development and social change. The security of energy supply under normal conditions does not now pose any serious problem — contrary to what was thought ten years ago. For the foreseeable future and for surely the 1980s, energy supplies are quite adequate to meet any growth in energy requirements. This is clear from the current state of market forces. The other aspects of the problem, concerning the stability of energy costs and the oil revenues for the OPEC countries, are both related to the stability of the oil market. The point which I want to make here is that OPEC oil is the indispensable residue in the world oil balance. Without OPEC oil there would be no world energy balance and no world oil balance.

Since 1980 the oil market has been subject to a series of pressures which have threatened the price structure. Many people thought that there would be a collapse in prices as a result of developments in the 1970s: a unique situation was created where demand for energy fell dramatically. The energy component of growth changed structurally. Moreover, the increased price of OPEC oil led to greater supplies of oil becoming available outside of OPEC. The oil price decided by OPEC has thus been subject to pressures both on the supply side and the demand side. These developments led to a dramatic fall in OPEC's share in world energy supplies and, more seriously, to some very serious financial imbalances. The oil revenues of OPEC countries, which reached a peak of about $US280 billion in 1981, fell to about $US150 billion in 1983. One can imagine the destructive effects of this fall.

Since the price reduction of March 1983, OPEC has been successful in stabilising the market. Prices have been holding fairly well, with the supply/demand balances being kept in a situation of equilibrium. I have, however, to warn against the precariousness of this stability, and its very serious impact on future energy balances. While market stability has been achieved, it is the OPEC countries which are paying the price. OPEC has been successful in holding the price simply by reducing its production. Other producers, such as the North Sea, Mexico and Egypt, have been in a different position. While they benefited a great deal from the OPEC price rise, in sustaining investments which otherwise would not have been made, they are also now benefiting from the OPEC retreat as a major supplier. They are continuing to offer for sale as much oil as they want to sell, at a lower price. So, in practice these producers (including the North Sea) are gaining a higher and higher share of a shrinking market. Yet the price structure from which they benefit is being held or defended only through OPEC's action in reducing its production.

In the long run the current structuring of world oil production could be a real source of instability. Against the falling trend of revenues, as a result of the fall in OPEC production and the reduction in OPEC's share of world energy supply, there is an increasing cost for development. It is clear that OPEC countries cannot go on reducing their share in the market, while other producers feel free to offer as much oil for sale as they wish. OPEC has strictly adhered to its price structure and its production programme so as to stabilise the market; without such action the market would be inherently unstable. Outside OPEC there should be some sharing of responsibility for market stability: this is an essential requirement for a healthy world energy economy and energy balance.

Dr El-Rumaihi

I have a few very quick remarks to make regarding the social and political constraints affecting the oil-producing states of the Gulf. Everyone knows that the states which compose the Gulf Co-operation Council are all governed by traditional regimes; the form of regimes is therefore different from that of most states in the Arab world — where regimes have emerged through revolutionary change. This is one aspect of the general political situation. The Gulf regimes have their problems and their successes, and one should be able to make a balance sheet assessing their performance. I want to mention now some items which should be placed on the balance sheet.

First, education. Thirty years ago we barely had any secondary schools. In some areas there were no schools at all until the early 1960s. Today the GCC states have twelve universities, so the governments have spent immense amounts of money on education at all levels. Even today, however, 50 per cent of all children under 15 in the GCC states do not have the opportunity to go to school. (The individual figures for Kuwait, the United Arab Emirates and to some extent Bahrain would be considerably more favourable than this.) The constraint is not money. It is in fact very difficult to build up a new educational infrastructure and to bring in the necessary teachers. Whatever the difficulties, a social problem evidently exists when 50 per cent of the children cannot go to school.

Second, the labour market — and specifically the role played by migrants. In Kuwait, 42 per cent of the total population are Kuwaitis and the remainder are non-Kuwaitis. Taking the working population alone, moreover, the percentage of Kuwaitis is even smaller. In Qatar and the United Arab Emirates the proportion of local people in the labour market is yet smaller. This constitutes an evident problem. As far as the Arab migrants are concerned, demand for them is usually high elsewhere. There is, therefore, a fundamental instability in the role which they play in Gulf economies. Most of the non-Arab migrants are uneducated and unskilled; many problems arise from a large migrant community of this nature.

Third, the political situation. Among the GCC countries, only Kuwait has an elected assembly. The others have not established any political channel for expression. You can imagine the problems which arise from this: people are educated, sent abroad for further education, and then denied a political channel through which to express the views they have developed. To my mind this is an ingredient to instability.

Fourth, the Gulf Co-operation Council experiment. Many good things have been said about the GCC, and it has indeed put forward some useful plans. Whether in economics or in politics, however, the GCC has great obstacles to overcome if it is to constitute a genuine channel for co-operation.

Finally, the Gulf war. In my view, an adverse turn to the Gulf war could affect the stability of the area much sooner than most people think. If Iran penetrated into southern Iraq, even for a week, very severe internal problems could develop within the states of the GCC.

Mr Belgrave

I thought it was very useful for Dr El-Rumaihi to remind us of the social and political aspects. There is, however, one aspect to the stability of the Gulf regimes which struck me two weeks ago during the visit of His Highness the Amir of Bahrain to this country. Western newspapers tend to speak about the Arab countries of the Gulf as a very unstable area; an area which could be contrasted in this respect with the highly stable regimes to be found in the Scandinavian countries and the UK. In point of fact, those are the only two groups of countries in the world which are still ruled by the same families that were ruling them 100 and 200 years ago. The families concerned have succeeded in adapting themselves to change and have produced the most startling example of stability.

I wish to focus now on what Dr Al-Chalabi has said. I agree that the oil price is fragile and that the present atmosphere of uncertainty is leading to a failure to make decisions on investments — a trend which could at some future date land us in renewed problems about supply. The reserves are there, but the decisions on investments are not being made. What, therefore, can be done to reduce uncertainty about prices? I think it is historically correct to say that attempts to manage markets among nations, or groups of producers, have only worked where there is a single dominant producer in the commodity concerned which is prepared — in its own interest and in the interest of all — to restrain its production. That, I suggest, was the situation in the United States oil market in the 1920s: it was the State of Texas which pro-rated its production, while Louisiana and the other states continued to act as they pleased. There was no formal agreement among them; in practice formal agreements break down. In the world oil market today it is OPEC, or rather Saudi Arabia, that is playing the role earlier played by Texas, while the other producers are obtaining a free ride. It still remains in the interests of all to stabilise the price.

Co-operation to bring about stability in the oil market is indeed desirable, but frankly I do not think there is any prospect of an agreement between producers and importers to this end. On neither side is there a group or an organisation which can negotiate an agreement or deliver it. We must, therefore, fall back on less formal arrangements, at least so that we do not do each other damage by mistake as we did most notably in 1979/80. Meetings like this do serve this purpose, but a day of discussion and dining together and then separating for a year does not really seem to be an adequate basis.

Chairman

I started this meeting on a fairly serious philosophical point and I wonder if I may just conclude it on a rather flippant philosophical point. I have sat through the day wondering to myself what in this room has symbolised in essence the nature of the meeting — most specifically our concern about the right price for oil. We all know the price of oil per barrel and how much oil goes into a barrel. When one considers how much a small bottle of soft drink costs, although it consists of only water, artificial sweetener, caffeine and preservatives, and one compares it with the price of oil, the question naturally arises: what is expensive and what is cheap?

INDEX

For Product Safety Concerns and Information please contact our EU
representative GPSR@taylorandfrancis.com Taylor & Francis Verlag GmbH,
Kaufingerstraße 24, 80331 München, Germany

Printed and bound by CPI Group (UK) Ltd, Croydon, CR0 4YY

08/05/2025

01864382-0005